Contents

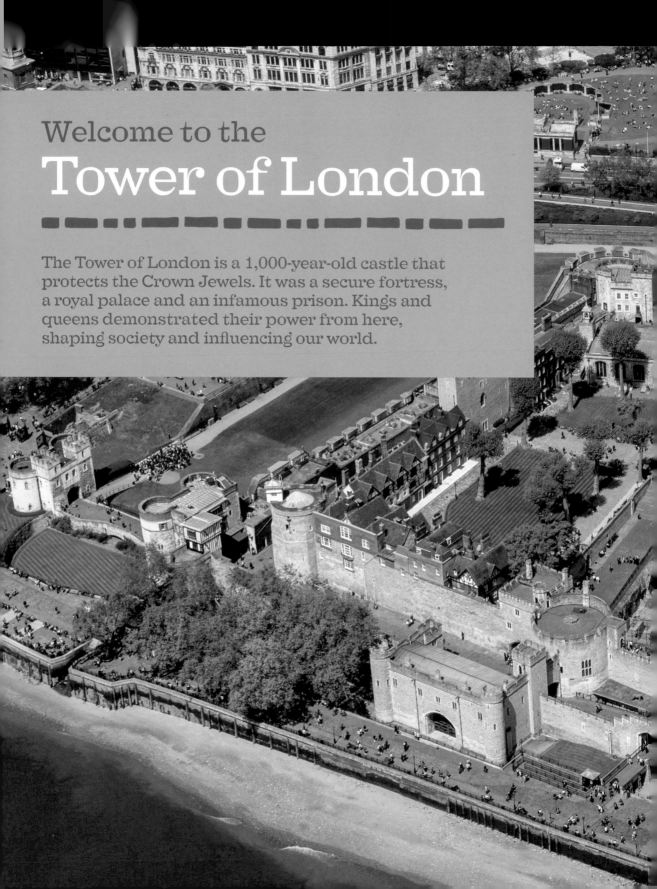

Welcome to the
Tower of London

The Tower of London is a 1,000-year-old castle that protects the Crown Jewels. It was a secure fortress, a royal palace and an infamous prison. Kings and queens demonstrated their power from here, shaping society and influencing our world.

Don't miss

There's so much to see at the Tower of London. Here are just a few highlights:

The Crown Jewels

No visit is complete without seeing this world famous collection housed in the Tower's secure vaults. Marvel at the fabulous gold jewel-encrusted pieces on display, most of them used at the coronation of a sovereign. These include swords of state, ceremonial maces and trumpets, as well as orbs and sceptres, coronation robes, and most famously, the magnificent crowns, some of which are still in use today.

The White Tower

This mighty castle keep was built by William the Conqueror in the 1070s to subdue and awe the local population, and it contains three fascinating floors to explore today. The White Tower was also a royal palace, once hung with rich tapestries and with every comfort installed, including garderobes (lavatories). You will enter through a magnificent hall once used for dining and entertaining. Enjoy the peace of the Norman Chapel of St John the Evangelist, once used for private worship by the royal family.

The Royal Armouries

Discover an extraordinary collection of arms and armour, curated by the Royal Armouries, within the White Tower. Visitors have been allowed to view the displays of weapons and equipment since at least the 1590s, so you'll be joining a historic tradition as you admire the famous armours of Henry VIII and the magnificent 'Line of Kings', thought to be the oldest museum display in the world.

The Battlements

Talk a walk around Henry III's huge defensive inner wall and imagine what it was like to defend the fortress against attack. Starting at the Salt Tower, you can explore nine towers on the way, including those once used as prison cells and still containing prisoner graffiti carved into the walls, such as this chart (detail above). In other towers, discover stories of the Tower Menagerie, the Peasant's Revolt and the Duke of Wellington.

The Fusilier Museum

The Royal Regiment of Fusiliers was founded in 1685 by James II to protect the royal guns within the Tower, two of which can be seen flanking the steps of the museum. Inside you'll find many fascinating objects from the history of the regiment, including Victoria Cross medals and an Eagle Standard captured during the Napoleonic Wars. Entry included in ticket price.

Yeoman Warder Tours

The Yeoman Warders (often called 'Beefeaters') have been at the Tower of London since the 14th century. Join one of their famously entertaining tours and enjoy 60 minutes of intriguing stories, secrets and bloodthirsty tales! For details of their guided tours (English only) and other free events, see the information boards on site.

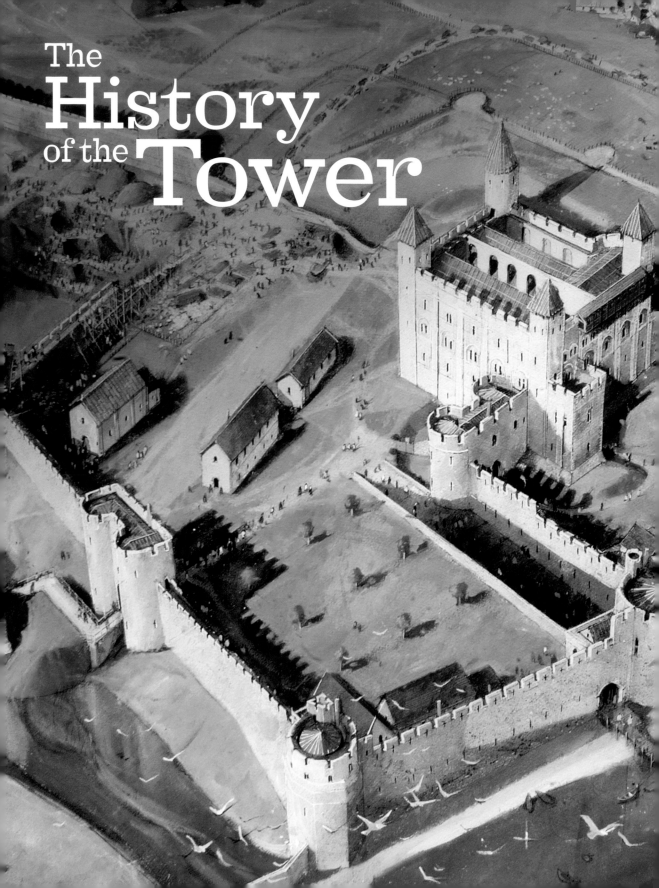

The History of the Tower

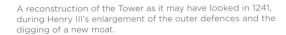
A reconstruction of the Tower as it may have looked in 1241, during Henry III's enlargement of the outer defences and the digging of a new moat.

William I as imagined by an unknown 17th-century artist.

During its long and colourful history, the Tower of London has taken on many different roles. As a formidable fortress it secured the Mint, armouries, where arms and armour were made and stored, and of course the Crown Jewels.

It was a royal palace for kings and queens and a home to a royal menagerie of wild and exotic animals, diplomatic gifts and trophies from wars and explorations abroad. It was also a notorious place of imprisonment for those who threatened national security. The castle itself has expanded in concentric rings, always with the mighty White Tower at its powerful heart. The plan on page 8 will help you understand the development of the site.

How the Tower developed

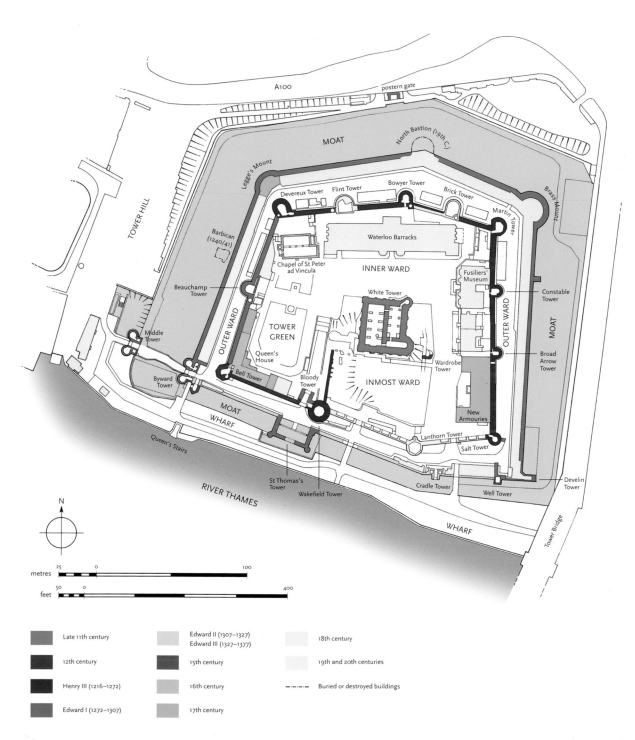

A100

postern gate

MOAT

North Bastion (19th C)

Legge's Mount

Devereux Tower

Flint Tower

Bowyer Tower

Brick Tower

Martin Tower

Brass Mount

TOWER HILL

Barbican (1240/41)

Waterloo Barracks

INNER WARD

Fusiliers' Museum

Chapel of St Peter ad Vincula

Beauchamp Tower

OUTER WARD

White Tower

Constable Tower

TOWER GREEN

Queen's House

Middle Tower

INMOST WARD

OUTER WARD

MOAT

Broad Arrow Tower

Byward Tower

Bell Tower

Bloody Tower

Wardrobe Tower

New Armouries

MOAT

WHARF

Lanthorn Tower

Salt Tower

Queen's Stairs

Develin Tower

St Thomas's Tower

RIVER THAMES

Wakefield Tower

Cradle Tower

Well Tower

WHARF

Tower Bridge

N

metres 25 0 100

feet 50 0 400

Late 11th century	Edward II (1307–1327) Edward III (1327–1377)	18th century
12th century	15th century	19th and 20th centuries
Henry III (1216–1272)	16th century	Buried or destroyed buildings
Edward I (1272–1307)	17th century	

Norman beginnings:
William and the White Tower

I t is with William the Conqueror (r1066–87) that the history of the Tower of London begins. In 1066 Edward the Confessor died childless, leaving several claimants vying for the throne. Edward's brother-in-law, Harold Godwinson, was crowned immediately but William, Duke of Normandy, a distant blood relative, said he too had been promised the throne.

William invaded and successfully defeated the English under King Harold at the Battle of Hastings. Heading for London – England's most powerful city – he laid waste to the surrounding countryside, terrorising the population. Seeing that the game was up, the city's leading men came to William to submit.

William's determination and faith in his own military might is reflected in the account of his biographer, William of Poitiers, who tells us that he sent an advance guard to London to construct a castle and prepare for his triumphal entry into the city. After his coronation in Westminster Abbey on Christmas Day 1066, the new king withdrew to Barking in Essex, 'while several strongholds were made ready in the City to safeguard against the fickleness of the huge and fierce population, for he saw that his first task was to bring the Londoners completely to heel'.

Archaeological evidence suggests one of these strongholds was built in the south–east corner of the Roman city walls, on the site of the future Tower of London. These early defences were soon replaced with a huge stone tower, which proclaimed the physical power and prowess of the new Norman monarch. This formidable castle keep was known as the 'Great Tower' until the early 13th century when Henry III ordered it to be whitened 'both inside and out', thus inspiring the name by which it is still known: the White Tower.

It is not clear exactly when work started on the Conqueror's White Tower or precisely when it was finished, but the first phase of building work was certainly underway by 1075. Gundulf, the new Bishop of Rochester was appointed as the Tower's architect. Norman masons were employed and some of the building stone was specially imported from William's native France. Labour, however, was provided by Englishmen. The Anglo-Saxon Chronicle comments in 1097 that 'many shires whose labour was due to London were hard pressed because of the wall that they built around the Tower'.

An iron age skeleton, probably dating from just before the Roman invasion, was excavated close to the Lanthorn Tower in 1976.

Roman invaders

In around 55 BC it was the Romans under Julius Caesar who were the invading force. Like their Norman successors they had been determined to impose their rule on the native inhabitants. London was their creation and the Normans were able to re-use parts of the existing Roman city walls (a standing section of the Roman wall can be seen preserved by Tower Hill underground station and within the Tower itself by the Ravens Shop). The riverside location was perfect for controlling access to London, and protecting against possible river borne attack.

By 1100 the White Tower was complete. Nothing quite like it had ever been seen in England before. The building is immense, at 36 x 32.5m (118 x 106ft) across, and on the south side where the ground is lowest, 27.5m (90ft) tall; the White Tower dominated the skyline for miles around.

The formidable castle keep was protected by Roman walls, parts of which can be seen today, on two sides, deep, wide ditches to the north and west and an earthwork topped by a wooden palisade (fence).

Although many later kings and queens stayed at the Tower of London, it was never intended as the main royal residence. Equally the Tower was not the first line of defence against invading armies, though it could rise to this challenge. The Tower's primary function was as a fortress and stronghold, a role that remained unchanged right up until the late 1800s.

A royal refuge and power base

King John depicted hunting a stag with his hounds.

As a power base in peacetime and a refuge in times of crisis, the Tower's fortifications were constantly updated and expanded by medieval kings. A series of separate building campaigns ensured that by about 1350, the Tower was transformed into the formidable fortress you see today.

These building works started in the reign of Richard I, the Lionheart (r1189–99). However, almost immediately after he gained the throne Richard left England on crusade. He left the Tower in the hands of his Chancellor, William Longchamp, Bishop of Ely who doubled the fortress in size with new defences.

They came just in time. In the King's absence his brother John seized the opportunity to challenge the Chancellor's authority and mount an attack. He besieged the Tower and its new defences held out, until lack of supplies forced Longchamp to surrender.

On his return in 1194 Richard regained control; John begged for forgiveness and was later named as Richard's successor. As king, John (r1199–1216) often stayed at the Tower and was probably the first king to keep lions and other exotic animals here (see page 58). His reign was characterised by political unrest; John made concessions to the barons by issuing Magna Carta in June 1215, but went back on his word as soon as he could. His opponents, who were in control of London and the Tower, invited Prince Louis of France to come and take the throne. Louis launched an invasion in 1216, but King John died suddenly of dysentery in the midst of fighting for his crown.

So at the age of only 9, John's son Henry III (1216–72) inherited a kingdom in crisis. However, within months the French were defeated at the Battle of Lincoln, and attention turned to securing the kingdom, with reinforcing the royal castles at the top of the agenda.

The boy King's regents began a major extension of the royal accommodation at the Tower, including the building of two new towers on the waterfront: the Wakefield as the King's lodgings and the Lanthorn, probably intended as the Queen's.

But when rebellious barons once again caused Henry to seek refuge at the Tower in 1238 the nervous King soon noticed the weakness of the castle's defences. He embarked on the building of a massive curtain wall on the north, east and western sides of the fortress, reinforced by 11 new towers and surrounded by a moat flooded by the Flemish engineer John Le Fossur (the ditcher).

Edward I used the castle as a secure place for storing official papers and valuables including diamonds and rubies, gold and silver church and banqueting plate, and various jewelled crowns and coronets.

This very public display of the King's power began to alarm Londoners. Contemporary writer Matthew Paris recorded their glee when a section of newly built wall and a gateway near the site of the Beauchamp Tower collapsed. Some said their guardian saint, Thomas Becket, had made a heavenly intervention. Evidence of one of the collapsed buildings was found during archaeological excavations in the 1990s.

King Edward I (1272–1307) was a more confident and aggressive leader who managed his country's rebels, but he was determined to complete the defensive works his father had begun at the Tower. Between 1275 and 1285 he spent over £21,000 (over £11m in today's money) on transforming the Tower into England's largest and strongest concentric castle (with one ring of defences inside another). Edward also commissioned a new riverside gate, St Thomas's Tower. Later known as Traitors' Gate, this served as the main water entrance for high status visitors as well as prisoners brought by river to the Tower to await their fate. In addition, Edward created another curtain wall enclosing the existing wall built by his father, and also dug a new bigger moat. In spite of all this work and building comfortable royal lodgings, he seldom stayed at the Tower.

Henry III at his first coronation in 1216.

However, Edward's reign saw the Tower put to uses other than military or residential. It was already in regular use as a prison (the first prisoner being Ranulf Flambard in 1100); and Edward used the castle as a secure place for storing official papers and valuables including diamonds and rubies, gold and silver church and banqueting plate, and various jewelled crowns and coronets. The King also moved coin production within the walls of the Tower, establishing what became the Tower Mint, an institution that was to play a major part in the castle's history until the 1800s (see page 44).

In contrast, Edward's son, Edward II (1307–27), lacking in both military skill and statesmanship, soon put the efficiency of the Tower's new defences to the test. The discontent of the barons reached a level comparable with his grandfather Henry III's reign, and Edward was often forced to seek refuge here. He took up residence in the area around the present Lanthorn Tower, and the former royal lodgings in the Wakefield Tower and St Thomas's then began to be used by courtiers and by the Wardrobe (a department which dealt with royal supplies, see page 38).

Unlike his father, Edward III (1327–77) was a successful warrior and the captured kings of France and Scotland were held at the Tower. He carried out minor building works at the fortress and extended the wharf, before Richard II (1377–99) shepherded in another period of intense domestic strife. In 1381 the peasants revolted and 10,000 rebels under Wat Tyler burnt and plundered the capital. An unarmed but determined group managed to enter the Tower after the King had ridden out to pacify the rioters (see page 35). Eventually, in 1399, Richard, accused as a tyrant by his cousin, Henry Bolingbroke, was forced to renounce his crown while he was held in the Tower.

For the defeated, the Tower was a place of murder and execution; victims included Henry VI in 1471 and the young Edward V and his brother in 1483.

Henry IV (1399–1413) was declared king the next day. His reign and that of his successor Henry V (1413–22) were quiet ones for the Tower, with very little building work or domestic unrest, but instability soon returned with Henry VI (1422–61 and 1470–1) and the Wars of the Roses.

During this struggle between the royal houses of Lancaster and York, the Tower was of key importance, and a place for victory celebrations. Henry VI held tournaments there; it saw splendid coronation celebrations for Edward IV (1461–70 and 1471–83) and victory parties for Henry VII (1485–1509), who entertained his supporters in grand style. However, for the defeated, the Tower was a place of murder and execution; victims included Henry VI himself in 1471 and the young Edward V and his brother in 1483 (see Murder at the Tower, on the following page).

Richard II was captured in 1399 and forced to hand over his crown to his cousin and usurper, Henry Bolingbroke in the White Tower, as depicted here. It's not known what happened to Richard after he was taken from the Tower to Pontefract Castle in Yorkshire. Some say he starved himself to death, others that he was starved. Shakespeare had him hacked to pieces in the second of his 'history plays'.

The young Princes in the Tower as imagined by a 19th-century artist, after Paul Delaroche.

Murder at the Tower

The disappearance and supposed murder of the two young sons of Edward IV remains one of the most intriguing stories of the Tower's history. After Edward's death in April 1483, his sons, 12-year-old Edward V and his 9-year-old brother, Richard of Shrewsbury, Duke of York, were taken to the Tower on the orders of their uncle, the Duke of Gloucester. The princes were declared illegitimate in July and their uncle was crowned King Richard III. What became of the princes remains a mystery; they were never seen alive again. Rumours of their murder spread quickly and became the inspiration behind Shakespeare's villainous portrayal of Richard III.

Then in 1674, two skeletons were found hidden under the staircase leading from the royal apartments to the Chapel of St John in the White Tower. Many people, including Charles II, considered them to be the bodies of the murdered boys, and the bones were re-buried at Westminster Abbey.

The skeletons were forensically re-examined in 1933. It was concluded that they belonged to two boys, aged about 10 and 12 years – the same age as the princes when they disappeared.

You can find out more about their story in the Bloody Tower, so named because of its traditional association with the princes' incarceration and murder. Many believe Richard III was the perpetrator – after all their disappearance undoubtedly helped him maintain his possession of the throne – but was it really that simple?

The Tudors:
The Tower as prison

The House of Tudor emerged triumphant under Henry VII, who built royal residential buildings at the Tower. Henry VIII (1509–47) continued the work begun by his father on a grander scale, erecting a large range of timber-framed lodgings, primarily for the comfort and enjoyment of his second wife, Anne Boleyn, ready for her coronation in 1533 (see page 51). But they were rarely used, and from this point on, the Tower ceased to be an established royal residence.

Henry VIII's decision to break with the Church in Rome swelled the Tower's population of religious and political prisoners from the 1530s onwards, while the country had to adjust itself to their monarch's new role as the Supreme Head of the new, Protestant Church of England. Prisoners included Sir Thomas More, Bishop Fisher of Rochester and two of Henry's wives. All four were executed.

Before his premature death, the adolescent Edward VI (1547–53) continued the political executions begun by his father. Mary I (1553–8) returned the country to Catholicism and her short reign saw many rivals and key Protestant figures imprisoned at the Tower. Potential rival claimants to the throne such as Lady Jane Grey and Princess Elizabeth were imprisoned at the Tower. Jane was executed on the Queen's orders in 1554; Elizabeth lived to be queen. As Elizabeth I (1558–1603) she continued the trend of using the Tower for high status and high security prisoners, but, like her successor James I (1603–25), she made few improvements to the Tower's defences.

Henry VIII continued the work at the Tower that was started by his father and had two of his wives, Anne Boleyn and Catherine Howard, executed there.

The Restoration:
The Tower and the Royal Ordnance

Charles II leaving the Tower and processing to Westminster Abbey for his coronation in 1661.

Charles I's reign (1625–49) ended in long and bloody civil wars (1642–9) between the King and Parliament. Once again the Tower was one of the King's most important assets. Londoners feared he would use it to dominate them but, in the end, the Tower was won by the Parliamentarians and it remained in their hands for the entire Civil War. Losing the Tower and London as a whole was a fatal blow to the King's forces and a crucial factor in Charles's defeat.

After the execution of Charles I in 1649, Parliament organised a great sale of the late King's possessions. Orders were issued to take all the Crown Jewels to the Tower Mint and 'cause the same to be totally broken, and that they melt down all the gold and silver and sell the jewels to the best advantage of the Commonwealth'. Oliver Cromwell, who became Lord Protector in 1653 installed the Tower's first permanent garrison, which succeeding monarchs used to quell trouble in the city.

With the restoration of the monarchy in 1660, Charles II (1660–85) planned ambitious defences for the Tower but they were never built. The Tower's use as a state prison declined and instead it became the headquarters of the Office of Ordnance (which provided military supplies and equipment). Most of the castle was taken over with munitions stores and offices and the Crown Jewels went on display for the first time – and in 1671 narrowly escaped being stolen (see page 43).

A programme of maintenance rather than building work characterised most of the 18th century; the existing fortifications were intermittently maintained and repaired. However, a new gateway and drawbridge were created at the east end of the outer southern curtain wall in 1774, giving access from the Outer Ward to the Wharf. Efforts were made to prevent the moat silting up, with little success.

Charles II commissioned a new set of regalia for his coronation in 1661, including the Sovereign's Orb, which is still in use today.

The Tower in the 1800s

Under the invigorating leadership of the Duke of Wellington, Constable of the Tower from 1826 until 1852, the moat, increasingly smelly and sluggish, was drained and converted into a dry ditch. After the Grand Storehouse burned down in 1841, the Duke ordered work to begin on a new barracks to accommodate a thousand men. On 14 June 1845 the Duke laid the foundation stone on the barracks named after his greatest victory – Waterloo.

The last time the Tower exerted its traditional role of asserting the power of the state over the people of London was in response to rallies and disturbances in the 1840s supporting Chartist demands for electoral reform. More defences were constructed, including a huge brick and stone bastion, but a Chartist attack never materialised. The bastion finally succumbed to a Second World War bomb.

Visitor figures increased dramatically in the 19th century; now it was not just intrepid and privileged sightseers who were paying for a guided tour as early as the 1590s, but ordinary people enjoying a day out. It was also at the beginning of this century that many of the Tower's historic institutions departed. The Royal Mint was the first to move out of the castle in 1810, followed by the Menagerie in the 1830s, which formed the nucleus of today's London Zoo. The Office of Ordnance was next to leave in 1841, and finally, the Record Office relocated in 1858, which became today's National Archives based at Kew.

The Duke of Wellington, first Constable of the Tower, painted by John Lucus c1837.

An increasing interest in the history and archaeology of the Tower led to a process of 're-medievalisation' in an attempt to remove the unsightly offices, storerooms, taverns and barracks and restore the fortress to its original medieval appearance.

Visitor figures increased hugely in the 19th century as ordinary people came to enjoy a day out.

In 1838 three of the old cages from the Tower Menagerie (closed a few years earlier) were used to make a ticket office where visitors could buy refreshments and a guidebook. By the end of Queen Victoria's reign in 1901, over half a million people were visiting the Tower each year.

The Grand Storehouse was completely destroyed by fire in 1841, and replaced by the Waterloo Barracks.

The new 'medieval' Tower

The way the Tower looks today is largely thanks to a 19th-century fascination with England's turbulent and sometimes gruesome history. In the 1850s, the architect Anthony Salvin, a leading figure in the Gothic Revival, was commissioned to restore the fortress to a more appropriately 'medieval' style, making it more pleasing to the Victorian eye – and imagination.

Salvin first transformed the Beauchamp Tower, refacing the exterior walls and replacing windows, doorways and battlements. Further commissions included restoring the Salt Tower (completed 1858) and making alterations to the Chapel of St John in the White Tower in 1864. Salvin restored the Wakefield Tower so that it could house the Crown Jewels (right), which remained there until 1967. In the drive to complete the perfect 'medieval' castle, his successor, John Taylor, controversially destroyed important original buildings to create uninterrupted views of the White Tower and to build a new southern inner curtain wall on the site of the old medieval palace.

The 1900s and beyond

Two World Wars saw the Tower back in use as a prison and a place of execution. Between 1914 and 1916 11 spies were held and subsequently executed in the Tower, including Franz Buschmann, who was killed by firing squad in 1915. The last execution at the Tower – of the German Joseph Jakobs – took place in 1941, the same year that Hitler's Deputy Führer, Rudolf Hess, was held there briefly, one of the last state prisoners at the fortress.

During the Second World War bomb damage was considerable, and a number of buildings were destroyed, including the Old Hospital Block in September 1940, and the mid-19th-century North Bastion, which was hit directly in October the same year. The moat was used for vegetable growing. The Crown Jewels were removed to a secret place of safety that has never been revealed.

Today the Tower of London is one of the most internationally famous tourist attractions and a world heritage site, attracting over three million visitors a year from all over the globe.

Second World War bombs destroyed large sections of the Old Hospital Block in 1940, as shown in this contemporary painting by William Hampton.

A Blast from the Past!

Photographers have been documenting the Tower since the late 19th century. These pictures from our archive offer an intriguing glimpse of life and changing times over the last 100 years.

Find these and many other fascinating pictures of the Tower at **www.images.hrp.org.uk**

1930

◄ Gun salute on Tower Wharf to mark the 20th anniversary of the accession of George V.

1930

▶ The Constable of the Tower, Lord Methuen (in feathered hat), Medical Officer, Colonel Rutherford (left) and the Major of the Tower, Lieutenant Colonel Burges, assemble for the ceremony of Beating the Bounds.

1924

◄ A bowler-hatted Ras Tafari (later Haile Selassie I, Emperor of Ethiopia) visited the Tower as part of a tour of Europe and the Middle East. He was crowned Emperor in 1930 and ruled (although he spent six years in exile) until 1974.

1929

▶ Yeoman Warders and Chelsea Pensioners enjoy a game of bowls at the Tower, with a trusty referee on hand to ensure fair play!

1897

▲ Soldier encampment in the north Moat, with Tower Bridge in the background. The Moat was often used as temporary accommodation for troops. These may have been the quarters for soldiers required for Queen Victoria's Diamond Jubilee celebrations in 1897.

1928

◀ Prince Potenziani, Governor of Rome, being shown around the Tower. During his visit to London he was conferred an OBE by George V. The group are pictured outside the Main Guard, built c1899 but destroyed by incendiaries in December 1940. The Bloody Tower is in the background.

1883

▼ The White Tower, looking north west, showing the demolition of the New Horse Armoury.

1946

◀ Yeoman Warders pose with two actresses from the film *London Town* in front of the Byward Tower. The film, which opened in September that year, starred many English actors and Cockney music hall stars.

The Tower as Fortress

The Tower of London – ancient, powerful and intriguing – is first and foremost an exceptionally secure military site. For centuries kings and queens have strengthened this iconic royal fortress for defence and attack at home and abroad.

The Tower is a visible symbol of the power of the State and of monarchy. When the mighty White Tower first rose up to dominate the skyline in the 1070s, Londoners in their low-roofed timber homes must have stood and stared in awe as the sound of hammers and chisels ringing on Caen stone rammed home the message that William the Conqueror was here to stay.

As later monarchs added huge defensive walls, battlements and further towers, flooded the moat and installed battalions of guards, the Tower was used as a central point to defend royal power and Britain's local, national and international interests.

The fortress acted as a nerve centre for the supply of England's armed forces at home and abroad, from 1066 to 1850. Thousands of weapons were made, tested and stored at the Tower, with its massive arsenal supplying the nation's armed forces. The Office of Ordnance (heavy weaponry such as cannon) was based at the Tower from 1700. Leading scientists, mathematics and craftsmen worked here and made the Tower a showcase for technical design.

With its impenetrable walls, massive gates and armed guards, the Tower was also the perfect safety deposit box for the nation. Kings and queens were reassured, knowing their money was safe in the Treasury, and royal valuables – clothes, armour, furniture and even food - were secure in the care of a section of the royal household based at the Tower, known as the Wardrobe. Monarchs also used the Tower as an archive to preserve documents of national significance.

For over 500 years, the Tower provided the perfect location for kings and queens to control the production of silver and gold coins in the Mint (page 44). Large amounts of precious metals, bullion and coins were stored here, and the tight security and terrible penalties deterred forgers.

The Mint and the Treasury are long gone, but the priceless Crown Jewels (page 40) nestle safely in heavily fortified vaults, guarded by members of the Regiment of Fusiliers and others who live in and serve at the Tower, along with the Yeoman Warders, once the monarch's private bodyguard.

Visitors to the Tower have enjoyed breath-taking displays of arms and armour for several centuries. The Tower was one of the earliest places to use weapons as decoration, and displays have been used to inspire both awe and fear, and for propaganda purposes, for most of its history. The spectacular Line of Kings (first displayed around 1625) was one of the earliest visitor attractions to use arms and armour to illustrate English history through mounted figures of important monarchs.

Henry VIII's 1540 armour.

Portcullis of the Bloody Tower, part of the inner defences.

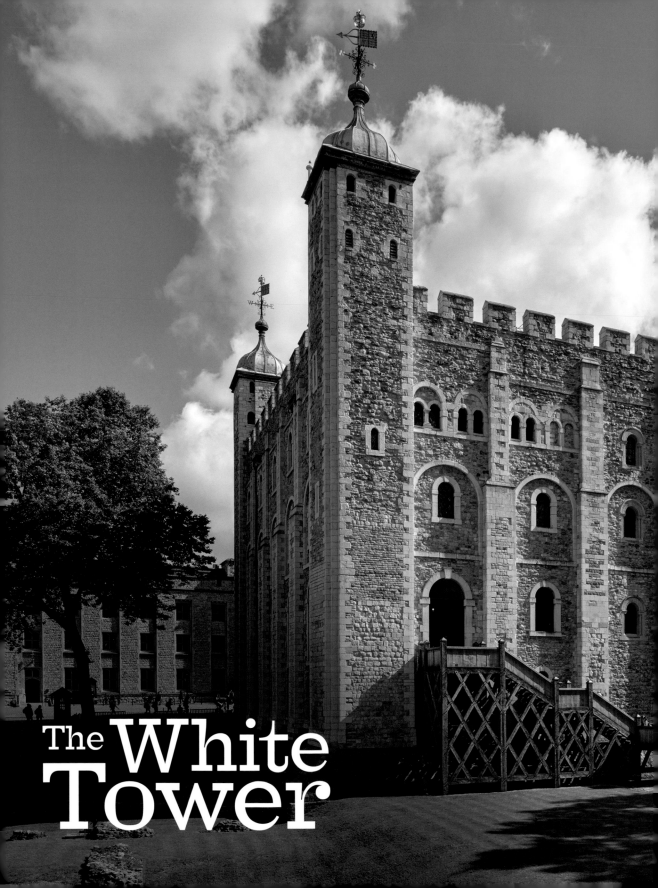

The White Tower

The wooden staircase in front of the mighty White Tower leads to a door well above ground level. The staircase could have been easily removed at times of attack. This staircase was created in 2015 to reflect the style of the original Norman builders.

If you stand at the foot of the mighty White Tower and look upwards it is still possible to understand the formidable power that this ancient castle keep was built to convey. When it was completed in c1100 the White Tower was the tallest building in London.

L ocal people must have watched the building rise from behind a forest of scaffolding poles with a mixture of awe and dread. The few who had travelled in northern France may have seen similar buildings at places like Doué-la-Fontaine and Ivry-la-Bataille, but for the majority whose lives took them no further than the countryside a few miles from home this tower was like nothing they had ever seen.

The White Tower is still an incredibly important building today. It is among the most complete and well preserved early-medieval secular buildings anywhere in Europe, a stirring example of how military architecture developed. It remains a potent and enduring symbol of authority and nationhood.

In the beginning

Construction of the White Tower began in the aftermath of the Norman invasion and the French victory at the Battle of Hastings in October 1066. We know, through archaeological tree-ring dating of timber found in the foundations of the White Tower, that the first stones were laid about a decade later in c1075-79 and that over the next 20-25 years building work progressed steadily.

The White Tower replaced the temporary timber fortifications that had been thrown up quickly by the invading Normans to consolidate their hold on London. Although the city had fallen quickly it remained an unstable threat to the new King. This great stone keep now proclaimed the permanence and power of the new royal dynasty. It was an impregnable building from which to exercise control over London and in which the King could stay when he visited the city.

The building work was overseen by Gundulf, Bishop of Rochester, a skilled architect who had come to England with the invading Norman army. He and the stonemasons with whom he worked designed the White Tower in the style of the castles of their native Normandy and imported stone from Caen with which to build it. There is some evidence of a short pause in the campaign of building work in the 1080s, perhaps caused by William the Conqueror's death in 1087 and the succession of his son, William Rufus, but they had probably completed the building by about 1100.

The exterior

The massive size of the building is striking. At each corner turrets project above the battlement. When the White Tower was new the turrets were capped with pointed roofs; in 1532 Henry VIII had these replaced by the elegant domes you see today. Three of the turrets are square, but the turret in the north-west corner is round to accommodate the building's main spiral staircase, which rises all the way from the basement to the roof. This round turret is known as Flamsteed's Tower after the 17th-century astronomer Sir John Flamsteed, who briefly used it as an observatory in 1675 (see box page 27).

The south-east corner of the White Tower is defined by the semi-circular projection that houses the apse (the domed recess) of St John's Chapel (see page 56). Its prominent inclusion in the design of the White Tower demonstrates that the building was both a secure military fortress and a grand domestic residence with refined architectural features.

Building work was overseen by Gundulf, Bishop of Rochester, a skilled architect. He and his stonemasons designed the White Tower in the style of castles from their native Normandy.

A well-defended palace

When first built, the White Tower contained two floors above a deep basement level. Each of the floors was divided by a wall, which split the building from north to south into two large chambers, and on the upper floor, an ornate chapel. A third floor was inserted in 1490 when the original roof was taken down and a new roof was built above it to accommodate the additional storey. Today if you stand in the final room of the top floor and look south towards the river, you can still make out the triangular outline of the former roofline on the stonework of the end wall.

The White Tower is entered via a wooden staircase that rises to a door well above ground level, adding to the dignity and the security of the entrance. The wooden staircase which you see today was constructed in 2015 using traditional carpentry techniques like those used by the original Norman builders. Wooden stairs like these could have been easily removed at times of attack. At such times the strong timber door that defended the entrance could also be barred from the inside, and the slots for the massive drawbar can still be seen on either side of the entrance.

> It is likely that the hall formed a great communal space where the court could dine and entertain.

The First Hall

The entrance leads into a vast hall which fills the whole western half of the building at this level. It is the first of a suite of chambers through which visitors to the White Tower have always passed. The precise original function of this hall and the other rooms on this floor is unclear. However, each is provided with a fireplace – some of the earliest in England and a new innovation in the 11th century – while the hall itself has a garderobe (lavatory) built into the thickness of the walls. It is likely that the hall formed a great communal space where the court could dine and entertain, while the slightly smaller room to the east of the spine wall was probably a more intimate chamber where the Keeper or Constable of the castle once lived.

This is the earliest known illustration of the Tower of London, dating from the late 15th century. London Bridge is shown in the background.

The King's Chambers

This layout of rooms is repeated on the floor above, but here the suite of chambers leads to the splendid and ornate Chapel of St John the Evangelist. This was the king's private chapel and its position on this floor suggests that these rooms were his own hall and chamber where he and his family lived and where he enacted the ceremonies of government. These rooms, which are also warmed by fireplaces and served by garderobes, would have once been richly furnished and hung with fine textiles. Before the roof was altered and the floor above was added in the 1490s these rooms would have been open to a splendid timber roof, which would have added to the sense of scale and magnificence.

There was no kitchen inside the White Tower and food had to be brought in from a great kitchen that once stood to the west of the building. It is not clear exactly by what route the servants brought food into the building but it is possible that there was once a door between the kitchen and the basement of the White Tower. The basement itself was probably always used for storage, since there are no fireplaces here to warm the rooms or on which to cook food. However, it does contain a deep well that would have sustained the occupants during times of siege.

This striking sallet of metal, gilt and bronze was made in Italy in 1470. A later owner added a luxurious lining of padded silk.

The White Tower as an Armoury

From the 14th until the 19th century the White Tower's main use was as a military storehouse and it was adapted accordingly. This use of the building has led to the role it serves today as a foremost museum of arms and armour, run by the Royal Armouries. Visitors have been allowed to view displays of weapons and equipment in the White Tower since at least the 1590s and from the 1680s it has held the magnificent Line of Kings, thought to be the oldest museum exhibit in the world. Many of the life-size wooden horses and armours still on display today in the White Tower date from this period.

Henry VIII's 1540 armour

This massive suit of armour creates a formidable presence in the First Hall of the White Tower. As a young man, Henry was slim and athletic; however, the once-trim King swelled in middle age as he became less active following a bad jousting fall. This vast armour was made for him in 1540 by the royal armourers in the King's Greenwich workshops in south-east London, with decorated gilt borders designed by Hans Holbein the Younger. It is a masterpiece of engineering that allowed the bulky

King to move easily and with maximum comfort. A particularly impressive feature, 'King Harry's codpiece', became famous in its own right when the Armouries were first opened to the public. The story was put about that if a childless woman stuck a pin into the codpiece she was more likely to conceive. Eventually the Archbishop of Canterbury intervened and the codpiece was removed as an incitement to superstition and ribaldry!

Storehouse and state prison

The White Tower's role as a royal palace did not last long. By the end of the 1100s new royal apartments and a large great hall had been built on the open ground to the south of the White Tower. Quickly the White Tower took on new roles. Its strength and size meant that it was the ideal place for storing treasure and important documents. From at least the reign of Edward I (1272–1307) parts of the White Tower were used for storing state papers and many were kept in specially made cabinets and cupboards in the Chapel of St John. These were only removed to more suitable storage in 1858 and now form part of the National Archives at Kew, south London.

The White Tower has a darker history. It was here that some of the most notorious prisoners were tortured...

The White Tower also acted as a prison for state prisoners. The earliest recorded was Ranulf Flambard, who escaped down a rope that had been smuggled into him in a barrel of wine in 1100. King John II of France (r1319–64) was held in relative comfort in the White Tower for several months in 1360 after his capture at the Battle of Poitiers, while the poet Charles, Duke of Orléans, spent part of his 24-year captivity here after the Battle of Agincourt in 1415. (See page 68 for more about famous prisoners).

However, the White Tower has a darker history as well. It was here that some of the most notorious prisoners were tortured (probably in the basement), including Guy Fawkes, and it may also have been the location of the feared solitary confinement cell known as Little Ease.

Astronomy at the Tower

Although hard to imagine today, in the 17th century the White Tower was still the tallest building in London. It gave the best unobstructed view of night sky, and so it was here that the first Astronomer Royal appointed by Charles II placed his telescope. John Flamsteed stayed at the Tower in 1674–5 to make astronomical observations.

He was working alongside his friend Sir Jonas Moore, a mathematician who was Master of Ordnance at the Tower. The men were part of a group of leading scientists and mathematicians (including Edmond Halley of later comet fame) who were trying to solve the problem of longitude (how mariners could pinpoint their position at sea) by observing the night sky. This was the key question of the era, vital for naval warfare and trade. Although Flamsteed's method ultimately didn't work, his research at the Tower underlines the importance of the fortress as a nerve centre and its impact on the world of science and exploration.

The Catholic Gunpowder Plot conspirators, 1605, led by Robert Catesby. After their plan to blow up Parliament was discovered, they were rounded up and sent to the Tower.

Robert Winter · Christopher Wright · Iohn Wright · Thomas Percy · Guido Fawkes · Robert Catesby · Thomas Winter

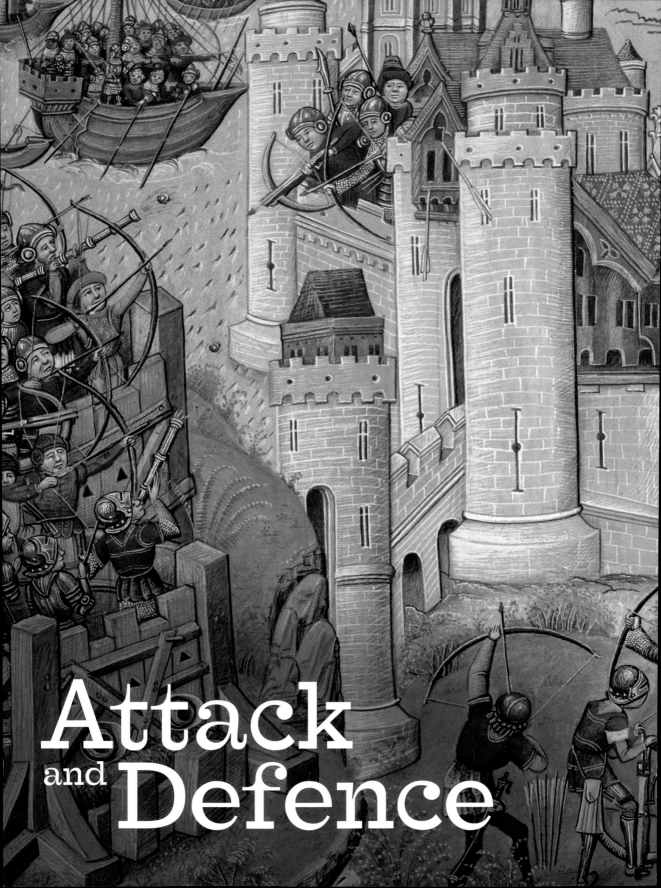

Attack
and Defence

This illustration from the 1400s depicts a castle under siege and shows the techniques and weaponry that would have been used against (or at least to threaten) the Tower of London in 1460 and 1471. To the left, the besiegers bombard the defenders on the battlements with arrows, handguns and cannon, shot from behind temporary timber defences.

A walk through the Tower's defences and a climb up and around the mighty Battlements is a great way to explore the Tower's different functions as a fortress, palace and prison.

Important visitors to the Tower in the late 13th century must have paused for a few moments in awe when approaching the impressive western entrance, built by Edward I (1272-1307) as part of his elaborate outer defences. The view from Tower Hill must have been magnificent: the stone Tower rising high over the surrounding wooden buildings, and Edward's new outer curtain wall reflected in the water-filled moat, which protected the three landward sides of the castle.

Making an entrance

The western entrance to the Tower was built between 1275 and 1281. It consisted of an intricate complex of three causeways and two drawbridges, a barbican (outer defence) that was later called the Lion Tower (now lost) and two twin-towered gatehouses, the Middle and Byward towers, which survive today. The whole of this complex was surrounded by a water-filled extension of the moat.

The Lion Tower

Visitors would have crossed part of the moat on the first of the causeways via a drawbridge to the Lion Tower, which took its name from the beasts kept there as part of the royal menagerie, (see page 60). You can still see the Lion Tower drawbridge pit, excavated in the 1930s. On the site stand a sculpted lion family that evoke the animals that would have roared at visitors, adding to the Tower's fearsome first impressions. This sculpture, by Kendra Haste, is one of several by the artist that you will see around the Tower, recreating the once-captive beasts.

The Middle Tower

Once over the first drawbridge, a second causeway and another drawbridge would have taken visitors to the fortified gatehouse, now known as the Middle Tower. Although the shape of the Middle Tower is 13th century, it was refaced in 1717, and the royal badge of George I now adorns the archway. This gate tower was once protected by archers, taking aim through the plentiful arrow loops and had two portcullis gates. You can still see the grooves for these in the passageway.

The Byward Tower

A final causeway leads towards the mightiest of Edward I's gate towers, the Byward Tower. The Byward Tower entrance passage is protected by two immense 13th-century cylindrical turrets, punctured by arrow loops. The northern turret also has a series of larger gun loops, reflecting developments in weaponry and defensive techniques.

Should any attacker manage to dodge the hail of arrows (and later, bullets) and get this far, they would have still had to breach the two portcullis gates. One gate still survives and can be seen overhead, as can the 'murder holes', intended to allow soldiers to douse fires lit by intruders (or some say for pouring boiling oil on their heads!). A groove for the second portcullis shows where it used to be.

Traitors' Gate

This is the most notorious of all the Tower's entrances. It's not hard to imagine the dread of those ill-fated prisoners such as Sir Thomas More and maybe Anne Boleyn, accused of treason, arriving here at the Tower. However, not all the history of this most grand of entrances is so grim. The timber framing above the archway, made by Henry VIII's Master Carpenter James Nedeham in 1532, is a memento of happier times for Anne Boleyn; it formed part of the excited rush to prepare the Tower for Henry's new queen. The timber framing was strengthened to support the big guns to be fired in celebration of Anne's coronation in June 1533.

This Watergate, then called St Thomas's Tower, was originally built for Edward I between 1275 and 1279. It was a daring variation on the traditional defensive gate tower. The arrowloops are discreet and the building had gilded window bars and painted sculpture on its exterior. Edward's luxurious royal barge could be moored beneath the great archway.

Water Lane

This part of the fortress was once under the river Thames. In 1275–85 Edward I achieved a major feat of engineering and reclaimed this ground. Building on hundreds of wooden piles, he pushed back the river and created the Outer Ward encircled by a new outer curtain wall. On the left is Mint Street where, until 1810, the majority of the nation's gold and silver coins were made, and where you can see the interactive exhibition 'The Tower's Mint: Coins & Kings'.

The Bell Tower

This ancient polygonal Bell Tower, originally lapped by the water of the Thames, is the second oldest tower in the castle after the White Tower. Built in the 12th century, probably for Richard the Lionheart, the Bell Tower is so called because the curfew bell has rung from it for at least 500 years to signal the closing of the Tower gates, although the current bell dates from 1651.

Between 1238 and 1241 over £5,000 (over £77m in today's money) was spent on building the curtain wall and towers, a great gateway, and on digging a moat.

Henry III's Watergate

The Bloody Tower gateway was built in the early 1220s as Henry III's river entrance, protected by archers and soldiers stationed in the lower chamber of the Wakefield Tower next to it. As king, Henry had a small private entrance on the other side of the Wakefield Tower, which allowed him to arrive discreetly and go straight to his royal apartments above. Traces of a staircase can still be seen. Around 1280, when the foreshore was infilled to create the Outer Ward, the gate became a land entrance into the Inner Ward. The gateway was extended and developed by subsequent kings and later became known as the Bloody Tower. The portcullis gate can be glimpsed overhead.

One of 'Edward III's lions', a dramatic wire sculpture by Kendra Haste, located near the Tower's western entrance. These amazing artworks commemorate Edward's original lions that once greeted visitors with fearsome roars!

The Battlements

This huge stone encirclement, defended by ten mural towers, was part of Henry III's fortification of the castle in the mid-13th century. Nine of these towers are open to the public and can be explored by walking around the battlements, starting from the Salt Tower.

Henry's reign was tumultuous and he needed the Tower to be strong for his own protection, and to present an impression of strength to his enemies. Between 1238 and 1241 over £5,000 (over £77m in today's money) was spent on building the curtain wall and towers, a great gateway, and on digging a moat. By 1285 these had been surrounded by Edward I's Outer Ward, outer curtain wall, and a rather more successful moat.

The inner curtain wall

This huge wall transformed the defences of the Tower. Archers and missile-throwing machines along the walls and within the mural towers had a good command of the land around the castle and could concentrate projectiles against an attack at any point. If the enemy managed to get on to or over the wall they were exposed to missiles from the mural towers and the White Tower.

The Inmost Ward

The Battlements on the south side were mainly built in the 1800s, destroying the remains of the rest of Henry III's lodgings. In the 1200s, these consisted of much more than St Thomas's and Wakefield Towers. These Battlements give a good view down onto the enclosed area in front of the White Tower, known as the Inmost Ward. This was once a busy complex of buildings set up to serve royal residence (see also page 50). These included kitchens and a great hall. The Inmost Ward was protected by the huge wall (the remains of which still survive behind the raven's cages), and the enormous Coldharbour Gate. The foundations of this building complex are to the left of the White Tower.

The Upper Salt Tower

This tower originally overlooked the Thames, and in times of trouble archers on the ground floor were able to protect it by shooting through the arrow loops. During peaceful times the ground floor of this tower was a storehouse for saltpetre, used for making gunpowder (hence its name).

The first floor chamber also has arrow loops but the original 13th-century chimney hood, and a large decorative window, give a sense of a more luxurious space. The heat from the fireplace would have kept Edward I's prisoner, the deposed Scottish king John Baliol, warm in the three years he was lodged here (1296-9). The convenient garderobe (toilet) is an added touch of comparative luxury.

Broad Arrow Tower

This tower is named after the 'broad arrow' symbol, which was stamped on goods to demonstrate royal ownership. This part of the Battlements demonstrates the function of the Tower to defend and guard valuables, and people, within its walls. The audio-visual displays here, and in the Constable Tower, reveal the specific occasion (the Peasant's Revolt of 1381) when attackers succeeded in penetrating the Tower's defences.

From the 1300s, the Broad Arrow Tower was connected to the government department responsible for royal supplies – the Wardrobe (see page 38). From Henry VIII's reign it was linked to the nearby Wardrobe Tower by a long storehouse, now demolished. As part of the Great Wardrobe, royal robes and valuable furnishings were kept here.

The Constable's Tower

The 19th-century Constable Tower is built on the site of one of Henry III's mural towers. It contains a model showing how the Tower would have looked in 1300 once Edward I had massively expanded his father's defences. The displays in the room and in the previous tower explore the story of the Peasants' Revolt of 1381 (see page 34).

'Sorcerer' Hew Draper's astrological chart from 1561.

Tudor prisoners

The Salt Tower's potential as a prison was exploited by the Tudor monarchy. Prisoners' graffiti is carved into the soft stone walls. An astrological chart by Hew Draper of Bristol, imprisoned on charges of sorcery in 1561, is one of the most elaborate. Many Catholic priests were imprisoned here during Elizabeth I's (1558–1603) reign – one such was the Jesuit Henry Walpole, who inscribed his name on the walls.

The Martin Tower

This part of the Tower has strong links with the Crown Jewels. Today, the jewels are kept in the Waterloo Barracks, but from 1669 until 1841, they were kept in the Martin Tower.

Today, this tower houses the 'Crowns through history' exhibition, which tells the story of historic royal crown frames that are no longer in use as crown jewels.

During the 200 years when this tower was known as the Jewel Tower, the Keeper of the Regalia and his family lived in the upper storeys, and the jewels were displayed on the ground floor, where the Jewel House shop is now.

The Brick Tower

The North Battlements were used to defend the Tower and guard weapons and soldiers. The Brick, Bowyer and Flint Towers are taller than the other towers, so as to command the rising ground beyond the fortress.

The Bowyer Tower

This tower became a location for the checking and finishing of small arms parts after the original workshops on the Wharf were closed. Fire broke out here in 1841, setting the whole of the Tower's Grand Storehouse (where the Waterloo Barracks is now) alight and threatening the whole fortress. A video installation tells this and other stories about the Duke of Wellington, who was Constable of the Tower at the time.

The Flint Tower

This last tower on the Battlements walk was originally a 13th-century mural tower in the inner curtain wall. The present Flint Tower was rebuilt after the 1841 Great Storehouse fire. It contains a display about the Tower of London's role as a propaganda machine during the First World War.

The Brick, Bowyer and Flint Towers are taller … so as to command the rising ground beyond the fortress.

The upper chamber of the Salt Tower. While this tower had an important defensive role, the fireplace and large window show this room was also meant to be lived in.

Anarchy at the Tower

In the foreground, the leader of The Peasants' Revolt, 1381. Wat Tayler is slain in front of young Richard II. The King is also shown addressing the heavily armed rebels.

During the Revolt, Archbishop Simon Sudbury was attacked while at prayer in the Tower chapel. He was dragged out and beheaded by the rebels on Tower Hill.

Astonishing scenes were played out in the royal apartments at the Tower in June 1381, when four hundred rebels stormed the fortress during the Peasants' Revolt.

William the Conqueror's White Tower and the huge curtain walls and towers of Henry III and Edward I cast a shadow of impregnable royal strength over London. But in reality, the Tower's fortunes as a defensive castle were somewhat mixed. Despite the strength of the fortifications, success depended rather more upon the loyalty and efficiency of its garrison, and the stocking of its weapon stores and food larders.

So when the Tower 'fell' In June 1381, it fell not to a well-organised army of knights, archers and skilled men with siege engines, but to a force of lower class rebels. This poorly-armed bunch didn't use sophisticated siege weaponry to breach this massive fortress - they simply ran through the gates, which had been left open!

A majestic portrait of Richard II, commissioned by the King himself, now hangs in Westminster Abbey.

The Peasant's Revolt

The revolt was sparked by a new tax that everyone over the age of 14 had to pay – the third new tax introduced in four years.

The rebellion began in the south east of England and quickly gathered momentum. A ten thousand strong force made up of freeholding farmers, skilled craftsmen and labourers marched on London to demand the heads of those they blamed for the tax. Oddly, they didn't blame the King, Richard II, for their suffering, and even professed loyalty to him while calling for the death of the 'traitors' who governed on his behalf.

The 14-year old Richard, his mother and royal household fled to the Tower as the rebels plundered and burnt the capital for two days. Eventually, the fortress came within the rebels' sights. Jean Froissart, a contemporary writer, described in his Chronicles what happened next...

The king had ridden out to meet the rebels at Mile End, just east of London. The Tower's drawbridges and portcullis gates had not been raised behind him, and a mob of at least 400 men stormed the castle. The men-at-arms guarding the Tower put up no resistance, and the peasants shook their hands as brothers and stroked their beards in a friendly fashion...

The rebels separated into gangs and ran through the Tower searching for 'traitors'. According to Froissart's account, although this is now disputed, they invaded the royal apartments and behaved with little restraint, several asking 'the king's mother ... to kiss them'. The Princess Joan, known as the 'Fair Maid of Kent' fainted at such familiarity and was carried to safety by her servants.

What is known is that the hunters' intended victim, the Archbishop of Canterbury Simon Sudbury was trapped at the Tower. As King's Chancellor and tax collector he was loathed. Realising that there was little hope of escaping, he chose to spend his final hours of life preparing for an untimely death. Caught praying in the chapel, the Archbishop was dragged out of the castle and on to Tower Hill. There he was beheaded on a log of wood. It took the headsman eight strokes before the 'traitor's' head could be impaled on a spike and mounted over the gate of London Bridge.

'You shall have no captain but me!'

The King later agreed to the rebels' radical demands for equality. Nevertheless, the tense situation quickly degenerated and their leader Wat Tyler was killed in the confusion. Showing remarkable courage, the teenage monarch rode forward and shouted 'You shall have no captain but me!' The rebels believed their demands would be met by their new champion and dispersed.

Richard's youthful valour had triumphed over the Tower's failure to protect his household. It would be a very different story 18 years later, when he returned as its prisoner, before losing his crown to the future Henry IV.

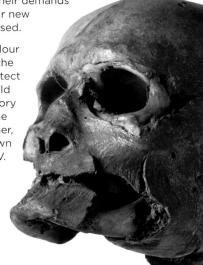

The decapitated head of Archbishop Sudbury, which was displayed on London Bridge.

The Tower Suffragette

Centuries after the Peasants' Revolt, the story of Leonora Cohen stands out among outbreaks of rebellion and protest at the Tower. Leonora was a suffragette member of the Women's Social and Political Union (WSPU) the militant group that had been founded by Emmeline Pankhurst. Their motto was 'Deeds, not Words'.

Leonora attacked the Tower on 1 February 1913 as a protest against women's inability to vote and the Act of Parliament that allowed the force-feeding of women who were on hunger strikes in protest. The Tower as a symbol of government and monarchical power (and arguably, male privilege) seemed a significant enough place to attack.

She concealed an iron bar under her coat, and gained access to the Crown Jewels, which at the time were housed in the Wakefield Tower. It was assumed she was a school teacher accompanying children, until she flung the bar at the display, smashing the case containing the insignia of the Order of Merit. A handwritten note wrapped around the bar read:

'Jewel House, Tower of London. My Protest to the Government for its refusal to Enfranchise Women, but continues to torture women prisoners – Deeds Not Words. Leonora Cohen' / (on reverse) 'Votes for Women. 100 Years of Constitutional Petition, Resolutions, Meetings & Processions have Failed'.

She was arrested by Yeoman Warders and taken to court, where she successfully represented herself and was released without charge. She remained a committed feminist until her death aged 108 in 1978. Her obituary in *The Times* fondly referred to her as 'The Tower Suffragette'.

Leonora Cohen, the 'Tower Suffragette' in 1910, and the Jewel House in the Wakefield Tower (top), which was used until 1967, when the Crown Jewels were moved to their present-day location in the Waterloo Barracks. Above: Leonora's WSPU dress that she made and wore to a ball in 1914.

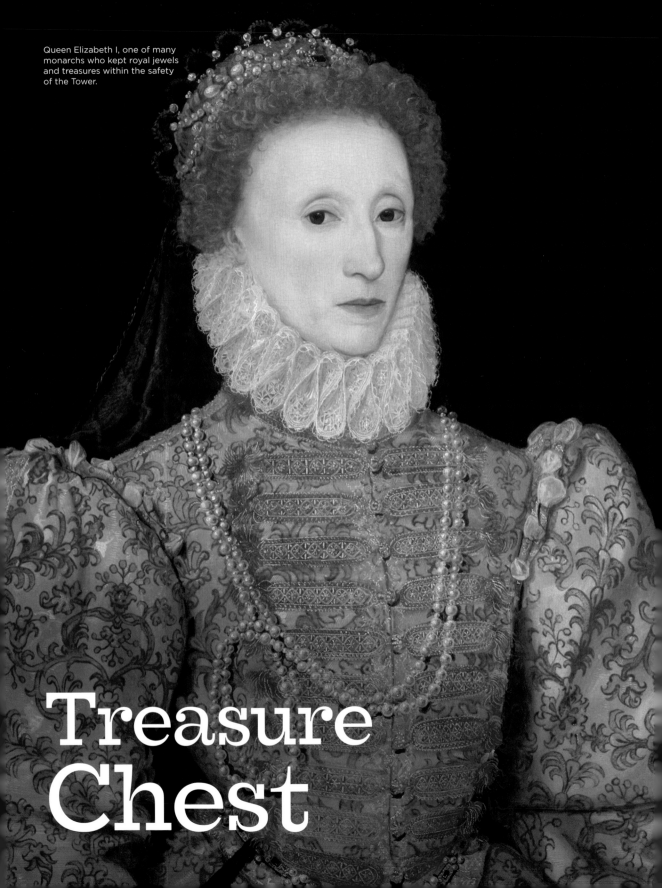

Queen Elizabeth I, one of many monarchs who kept royal jewels and treasures within the safety of the Tower.

Treasure Chest

As a secure fortress, the Tower of London was an ideal place to keep precious items safe, as well as keeping enemies out. As the nation's 'treasure chest', the Tower was where kings and queens kept their valuable personal possessions, and where items of national importance were stored.

Royal Treasures

Medieval monarchs needed to project an awe-inspiring public image at all times. They dressed themselves in silks and furs, wore gold crowns and jewel-encrusted ornaments and dispensed wisdom and justice from impressive thrones set in highly decorated rooms. Walls were covered with richly woven tapestries, floors with brightly coloured tiles, and food was served on golden plates. The challenge for their servants was maintaining this splendour while travelling. Kings and queens spent a lot of time on the road, seeing their country and being seen by their subjects. It took a dedicated department - the Wardrobe - (and a lot of storage space) to ensure their clothes, jewels, food, armour and furniture were available wherever the sovereign was staying.

The Wardrobe

In the reign of Edward I (1272-1307), the Wardrobe was the most powerful department in the Royal Household - in charge of recording and storing most of the king's personal wealth: from clothes and armour to furniture and food.

The Wardrobe department moved with the monarch but had two permanent stores at the Tower of London and at Westminster Palace. However, all valuable items were moved to the more secure Tower, after a robbery at Westminster in 1303. The sacred and highly symbolic regalia stayed under the protection of the monks at Westminster Abbey.

In the late 1300s, a specialist department called the Privy Wardrobe developed out of the Wardrobe. Its job was to produce, store and supply arms and armour for military campaigns, as well as the king's own personal armour. In the later 1600s this split into the Armoury and Ordnance departments which remained at the Tower until the mid-1800s.

The Treasury itself

Over time, other sections of the Wardrobe became departments in their own right. The Treasury looked after items of high value such as jewels, coronation regalia, precious metal tableware and of course, the monarch's own money. The Crown Jewels are at the Tower of London today because of the Tower's historic role as a Treasury, and because it remains a secure fortress that can keep the coronation regalia safe.

Detail from the Wine Cistern made for George IV in 1829. It is also known as the Grand Punch Bowl when filled with the contents of 144 bottles of wine!

The Crown Jewels

The Sovereign's Orb, (detail) 1661. This is placed in the monarch's right hand during the coronation ceremony. The Orb retains many of its original 17th-century gems, including most of the 365 rose-cut diamonds.

No visit to the Tower is complete without seeing this world–famous collection.

Most of the fabulous gold and gem–encrusted pieces on display in the Jewel House are those objects used at the coronation of a sovereign and are collectively known as the Coronation Regalia.

These include swords of state, trumpets and ceremonial maces, as well as coronation robes, but probably the most famous items are the stunning crowns, some of which are still in use today.

After the execution of Charles I in 1649 the royal regalia were almost totally destroyed on the orders of a vengeful Oliver Cromwell. The only items to survive are three 17th-century ceremonial swords, and a 12th-century Coronation Spoon used to anoint the monarch with holy oil.

After the restoration of the monarchy in 1660, Charles II ordered a splendid new set of jewels. The most recent objects on view today were made in 1953 for Queen Elizabeth's coronation.

Sent to the Tower!

Until 1649 the special and sacred items of Coronation Regalia were kept at Westminster Abbey, while 'everyday' crowns, royal jewels and treasures travelled with medieval monarchs and were kept in strongrooms at their palaces.

However during Edward I's reign (1272–1307) thieves broke in to the Abbey and made off with a stash of royal treasure, fortunately missing the regalia. It was decided that royal valuables would be far more secure if locked up at the Tower of London, so they were moved to the basement of the White Tower, although the monks of Westminster insisted the sacred coronation items must remain at Westminster Abbey.

The new regalia made for Charles II in 1661 were kept at the Tower after his coronation. The Crown Jewels went on display to the public in 1669 in the Martin Tower, when, astonishingly, visitors were allowed to handle them on payment of a small fee to the Jewel House Keeper! It seems hardly surprising that they were nearly stolen in 1671.

Today the Crown Jewels are securely housed in the Waterloo Barracks, built in the 19th century on the site of the Grand Storehouse, which was destroyed by fire in 1841.

Dazzling diamonds

The Crown Jewels incorporate some spectacular precious stones, including two magnificent diamonds: Cullinan I (the First Star of Africa) set in the Sovereign's Sceptre with Cross, is the largest top quality cut diamond in the world, weighing just over 530 carats. The legendary Koh-i-Nûr diamond from India is set in the Crown of Queen Elizabeth The Queen Mother.

The Sovereign's Sceptre with Cross (detail), 1661, which was transformed by the addition of the magnificent Cullinan I diamond in 1910.

Royal rings

During the final part of the coronation ceremony a ring is placed on the monarch's fourth finger of their right hand. The Sovereign's Ring, 1831, was made for William IV's coronation in 1831, with rubies forming the cross of St George (the patron saint of England) on a large sapphire. The Queen Consort's ring, 1831, belonged to William IV's consort, Queen Adelaide.

Hard working crown

Queen Elizabeth II was crowned with St Edward's Crown, which was made in 1661, but modelled on the lost medieval crown of English kings, named after King Edward the Confessor (1042–66). At the end of the ceremony it is traditionally exchanged for the Imperial State Crown, which is set with some of the most famous diamonds and gemstones. It is this crown that The Queen wears at the State Opening of Parliament.

The Imperial State Crown contains:

- ▼ 2,868 diamonds
- ▼ 17 sapphires
- ▼ 11 emeralds
- ▼ 5 rubies
- ▼ 273 pearls

Admire beautiful crown frames and discover how crowns developed in the 'Crowns Through History' exhibition located in the Martin Tower.

Discover more detail about the Crown Jewels in The Crown Jewels souvenir guidebook, available in Tower of London shops or online at **www.historicroyalpalaces.com**

In 1669 visitors were allowed to touch the jewels, after handing a small donation to the Jewel House Keeper!

'Stop, thief!'

'Colonel' Thomas Blood

Early in the morning of 9 May 1671, Thomas Blood, an Irish soldier, arrived at the Tower of London with three companions: his son Thomas, Robert Perot and a thug called Richard Halliwell. All were secretly armed with knives, pocket pistols and swordsticks. They tied up and gagged Talbot Edwards, the Keeper of the Crown Jewels, then stabbed and beat him about the head when he struggled. With Edwards immobilised, the three men seized crowns, the orb and the sceptre, but just as they prepared to make their way out of the Tower, fate intervened in the form of Talbot Edwards's son. Having been abroad for several years, he returned home unexpectedly and raised the alarm. The thieves tried to make their escape but, after a brief scuffle in which shots were fired, they were overpowered and captured.

Blood was an intriguing and complex character. He was a reckless, violent adventurer, who had seen some military service, but his rank of 'Colonel' was purely of his own invention. Exactly why he wanted to steal the Crown Jewels is not clear. Whatever his reasons, rather remarkably, Charles II pardoned him.

The Mint and Records Office

Edward I groat, 1279.

The institutions of the Mint and the Records Office were essential to transforming the symbolic power of the sovereign into real control over everyone's daily lives, and were kept secure within the Tower's walls.

Making Money

Money makes the world go round – and a mint is the place where money is made. The Tower's Mint made the majority of the country's coins for over 500 years.

In 1279, King Edward I's currency was in crisis. Coins were worn out and many had been damaged by years of 'clipping' – shaving off slivers of metal to melt down and sell. The King needed to keep a closer eye on production, so he moved the coin-making workshops from the City of London into the heart of his London fortress. Over the next 500 years, kings and queens struggled to maintain a tight grip on the financial health of their kingdoms through making new coins at the Tower of London and smaller mints around the country.

Fighting forgery

Silver and gold coins were high-security items, but even more valuable were the dies that were used to produce them, which stamped the design into the precious metals. If those dies fell into the hands of counterfeiters, criminals would be able to fake coins and destabilise the whole economy.

Coin forgery was, therefore, considered treason, and those caught faced execution or deportation. It was the job of the Mint Warden, a post held between 1696 and 1699 by famous scientist Isaac Newton, to seek out and prosecute forgers.

Luckily for the Mint, Newton was as good at detecting coin criminals as he was at devising scientific theories. Many counterfeiters were hanged for their treasonous crimes, while Newton was rewarded with the more lucrative job of Master of the Mint, which he held until his death in 1727.

The Mint left the Tower in 1810 for a new home in a purpose-built factory on Tower Hill nearby. It outgrew this factory in the 1960s and moved to South Wales, where it still makes British coins today.

The first gold sovereign was minted at the Tower in 1489.

Charles II commemorative silver medal c1667.

In 1797 a severe currency shortage meant the government had to circulate foreign coins, countermarked at the Mint with the head of George III.

Below: Elizabeth I had her father's debased currency made into new purer coins at the Mint, bearing her portrait.

Life for Mint workers up until the 1600s was hot, dirty and dangerous as the coins were produced by hand. Many men lost fingers or eyes, until the introduction of faster, safer screw-operated presses, like the one in this engraving of 1750.

A National Archive

As a Records Office for storing documents of national significance, the Tower held a vital role in preserving traces of the nation's history. These included charters, laws and accounts that recorded exchanges of land, legal decisions and financial transactions. These documents were written on animal skin parchment, rolled up and stored securely at the Tower of London from at least the 1200s.

The records were used largely by lawyers until the 1700s. Then the growing fashion for historical research meant they got more use from antiquarians digging into the country's past.

A 'deplorable pickle'

Space was always a problem at the Tower, as different departments competed for storage. The Records Office struggled to find enough room for their expanding collection and by the 1660s, most of the records kept in the Upper Wakefield Tower were in a 'deplorable pickle' according to Keeper of Tower Records, William Prynne. A new space was needed, and by 1707 the Chapel of St John in the White Tower had been converted to hold records rather than church services.

Fire!

Fire was an ever-present danger at the Tower, and the records narrowly avoided disaster when a nearby ordnance building burnt down - nearly taking 1,000 years of history with it.

However, by the 1800s, the government was calling for all government records to be stored in one place, so the Tower records were moved to a Public Record Office near the centre of London's law district in Chancery Lane. The records were moved again to a purpose-built storage and access building in Kew, London by 1998, their home today.

The Record Office in the Upper Wakefield Tower in 1801.

The Tower as Palace

Seen from outside, the Tower appears only to be an austere and forbidding fortress. Surprisingly, it is also a royal palace, once used by kings and queens who enjoyed astonishing standards of comfort and luxury, equivalent to their other palaces.

From Henry III (r1216–72) to Henry VIII (r1509–47), monarchs built highly-decorated, richly-furnished accommodation for themselves and their families within the Tower's protective stone walls. The rooms were comfortable, impressive, and designed to show off their power and status. Even when kings and queens were elsewhere, these prestigious rooms were used by royal officials who governed in their place.

The towers of St Thomas's, Wakefield and Lanthorn formed an interconnected palace (see page 53); today the spaces re-create royal life during the reigns of Edward I (r1272–1307) and his father Henry III. A sense of the magnificence and grandeur is suggested by the luxurious fabrics and paintings of Edward's bedroom, and the decoration of Henry's throne room and small chapel.

Chapels royal (see page 56) were an integral part of the royal palaces, used by kings, queens and the Tower community. St Peter ad Vincula is the Tower's parish church, and last resting place of several famous prisoners executed here, including two of Henry VIII's wives. The breathtakingly beautiful, austere Norman Chapel of St John in the White Tower was once used by the royal family for worship, with the monarch seated on a throne.

Monarchs demonstrated their status through conspicuous consumption of the most expensive items, and at the Tower, some of the most bizarre. A menagerie (see page 58) of lions, tigers, elephants and other exotic beasts, including a polar bear, lived out uncomfortable and short lives here. Many were given as exotic presents to the English sovereigns.

Sadly, the most palatial of the Tower's royal apartments vanished in the 18th century. Now only the famous ravens strut over the grass beneath which lies the remains of Henry VIII's magnificent Tudor palace (see page 48). Before his marriage to Anne Boleyn,

the love-struck King lavished money on the existing old-fashioned royal buildings to provide luxurious pre-coronation accommodation for his new queen. As monarchs had done for hundreds of years before her, Anne set out in triumph from the Tower to Westminster Abbey before her coronation, only to be imprisoned in the same rooms just three years later before her execution.

Now the onion-shaped domes on top of the White Tower are the last remaining vestiges of Henry's massive spending spree and short-lived happiness with Anne. But after hundreds of years, the unique ceremonies and traditions that are still observed, such as the Ceremony of the Keys, Constable's Dues and the regular thundering gun salutes on the Wharf (see page 62) underline the Tower's importance as a palace and the ideal place to demonstrate royal power.

Left: The replica of Henry III's throne in his son Edward I's Wakefield Tower is based on the Coronation Chair in Westminster Abbey.

Right: This 13th-century manuscript of Edward I and his court shows the richness of the decoration and furnishings of a royal palace.

TOWER HILL

The Posts of the Scaffold

Postern Gate

The Tower between the Church Yard and the Hill are S.ᵗ Katherines Roode

AH

The Iron Gate

The Bulwark Gate

The Lyons Tower

The Lyons Gate

A

B

C

D

E

F

G

H

The TOWER of LONDON

W

X

The Lieutenants Lodgings

Jewel House

The Hall decay'd

THE WHARFE

RIVER THAMES

The Lost Palace

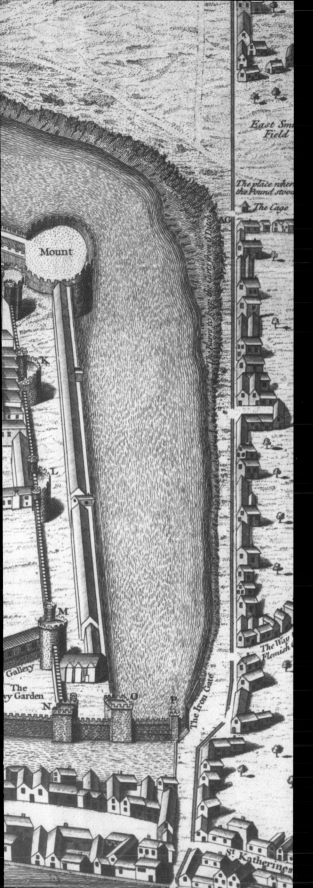

The following text labels appear on the plan:

East Smithfield

The place where the Pound stood

The Cage

Mount

K

L

M

Galley

The Way Garden

N

O

P

The Iron Gate

The Way Flemish

St. Katherines

A plan of the Tower from around 1597 gives a detailed record of many of the medieval and Tudor buildings that were swept away or drastically modified in the 17th century, notably the royal lodgings and the Great Hall (already described as 'decay'd') to the south of the White Tower.

Below the lawn in front of the White Tower are the remains of a royal palace where Henry VIII (1509-47) and Anne Boleyn (1533-6) celebrated their coronations and where Anne spent her final days in prison.

The area to the south of the White Tower had long been used by the kings of England for their palace. Royal apartments probably already existed here by the beginning of the reign of Henry III (1216–72) but he rebuilt them and extended them in the 1220s and 1230s. This complex of buildings was enclosed behind a new gatehouse tower, the Coldharbour Gate, which provided security and seclusion from the rest of the castle.

Today when you stand by the ruins of the Coldharbour Gate imagine peering through a gateway and glimpsing the porch of the Great Hall across an open courtyard beyond. These buildings were to form the core of the Tudor palace, where Henry VIII and his new wife Katherine of Aragon first stayed on the night before their coronation procession in 1509.

Pimping up the palace

By the early 1530s, Henry VIII was tiring of Katherine of Aragon, and was determined to have a new queen to give him a longed-for son. The spotlight turned again to the Tower, as teams of builders and craftsman descended during the summer of 1532 so that the palace could once again play its part in a moment of national importance – the coronation of Henry's second wife, Anne Boleyn in 1533.

Henry's old rooms were modernised and refurbished. At the same time the roof of the Great Hall was repaired and the whole building was given a lick of yellow paint. On top of the White Tower the four iconic onion domes were built to replace older, dilapidated cone-shaped roofs that had crowned the White Tower since it was first built. In the King's and Queen's gardens new ornamental bridges adorned with vanes and statues of royal heraldic beasts were constructed.

The end of an era

By the 1660s the palace had fallen completely out of use and permission was granted to demolish it and build new ordinance storehouses and offices in its place. Although parts of the royal palace were incorporated into some of the new buildings, these were later swept away in further demolitions and rebuilding works during the 18th and 19th centuries. The Lanthorn Tower which housed the King's bedchamber was destroyed by fire in 1774. The current Lanthorn Tower was rebuilt on the same site in 1883. Today all that remains of the magnificent lost Tudor palace are fragments of archaeology below the lawn.

The Family of Henry VIII (detail), painted around 1545 by an unknown artist, is of an imagined interior, but gives an idea of just how sumptuous the Tudor royal apartments at the Tower might have been.

Anne Boleyn at the Tower

Anne Boleyn was nearly 33 years old when she became Henry VIII's second wife and queen consort in 1536 and she was already pregnant with Henry's child. The baby that she carried on that day would grow up to become Queen Elizabeth I (r1558–1603). Henry and Anne were finally married in a secret ceremony at Whitehall Palace in January 1533 and she was officially recognised as queen on 12 April of the same year. Six weeks later she was crowned in Westminster Abbey.

The Coronation

The formal celebrations of Anne's coronation lasted for four days and were followed by jousts and pageants. On Thursday 29 May the festivities began with a river pageant that brought Anne from Greenwich to the Tower in a flotilla of boats and barges. At the head of the flotilla was the Mayor of London's barge on the deck of which had been built a spectacular model of a dragon 'continually moving and casting wildfire'. On board were trumpeters blowing fanfares and gunners firing salutes in celebration.

The river pageant escorted Anne to the Tower wharf where she disembarked from her barge. Henry was waiting to meet her and he greeted her with a kiss. Together they entered the Tower to spend the evening and the following day in celebration.

On the Friday Henry and Anne feasted in the gleaming new palace. The following morning, Anne processed through the City of London to Westminster Hall, watched by crowds of Londoners, cheering (with some booing) as she passed by in her horse-drawn litter. Anne was entertained along the route by short plays, pageants and choirs of schoolboys.

> On Thursday 29 May the festivities began with a river pageant that brought Anne from Greenwich to the Tower in a flotilla of boats and barges.

Imprisonment and trial

The celebrations did not last for long. By 1536 Henry was becoming frustrated again. Anne had failed to provide him with a male heir. Henry already had his eye on his next wife, Jane Seymour, and so encouraged by powerful men amongst his advisors with whom Anne herself had clashed he determined to rid himself of her.

Anne was arrested and brought by barge to the Tower on 2 May 1536. The charge against her was one of treason founded on allegations of adultery and incest. Just as she had done three years earlier Anne landed at the wharf and entered the Tower. But this time she was met by the Constable of the Tower, Sir William Kingston.

Anne was kept in the Tower for two weeks before her execution on 19 May 1536. Those two weeks were punctuated by rounds of questioning by her gaolers until on 15 May she was brought to trial in the Great Hall of the Tower, which had had to be hastily set up as a court room.

Execution

Anne was found guilty and condemned to death. Four days later on a scaffold erected outside on Tower Green her head was cut off by the sword of a French executioner. Her body never left the Tower but was buried beneath the altar in the Chapel of St Peter.

A portrait of a woman thought to be Anne Boleyn, by an unknown artist, c1533–36.

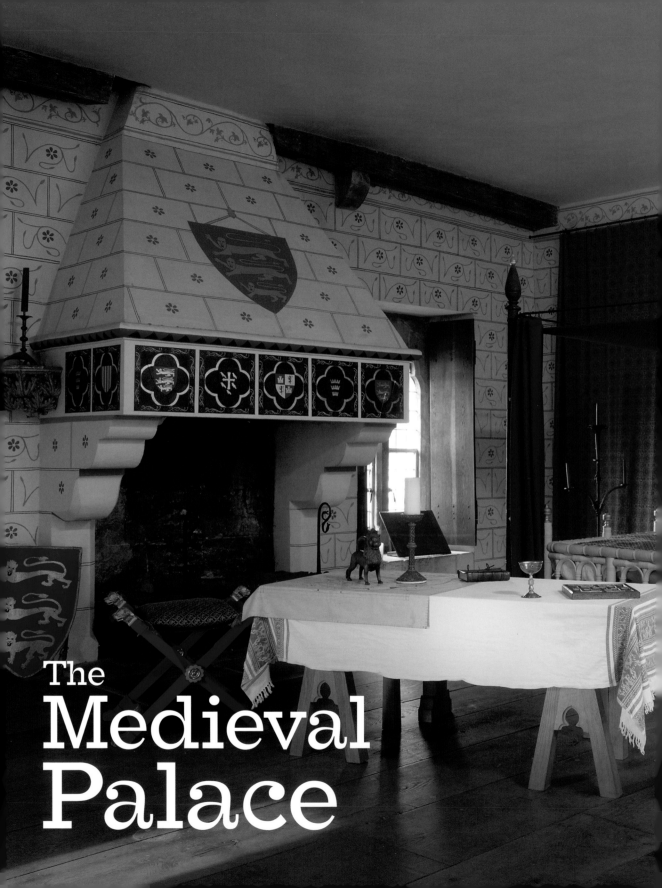

The Medieval Palace

The royal bedchamber inside St Thomas's Tower, re-presented as it might have appeared in the time of Edward I. The specially-large bed was made to accommodate the tall, imposing king, nicknamed 'Longshanks'.

Edward I and his beloved queen, Eleanor of Castile, from a 14th-century chronicle of his life.

Here are lodgings fit for a king, surprisingly comfortable and presented to give a glimpse of life during the reigns of medieval monarchs Henry III and his son Edward I.

St Thomas's Tower, the Wakefield Tower and the Lanthorn Tower are today known collectively as 'the Medieval Palace'. They lay at the heart of what was formerly the residential area of the Tower, richly decorated and comfortable lodgings, grand enough for any medieval monarch. Built by Henry III (1216–72) and his son Edward I (1272–1307), they have been re-presented for today's visitor to evoke a vivid picture of 13th-century life.

Short stay

Medieval monarchs never stayed at the Tower for very long, and it was usually for a specific purpose rather than pleasure, although the palace had to be fit for royalty, even for short visits. Edward I, for example, only stayed here for 53 days in 35 years of rule.

St Thomas's Tower

St Thomas's Tower was built by Henry III's son, Edward I, between 1275 and 1279. The wharf that now separates this tower from the Thames had not been built in the 13th century, so Edward's building looked out directly on to the river. Its impressive façade declared to river travellers the magnificence of this warrior king.

The first large room, one of two – which later records describe as a 'hall with a chamber' – has been left unrestored. This was where the King could dine and entertain. Many people have lived in St Thomas's Tower since Edward's day, and the archaeological evidence for that, such as timber framing, a staircase and wallpaper, is preserved in this room. Remains of the hall's original 13th-century fireplace, a garderobe (lavatory) wall and a picturesque vaulted turret still survive.

A short film explores the how Henry III and Edward I each used the Tower. Edward mostly stayed to supervise building work and prepare for war, whereas his father sought shelter behind its strong walls from rebellious barons. Both kings extended the Tower's defences considerably.

A king's bedchamber

Edward I's bedchamber may seem a little bright for modern eyes. Its furnishings have been reconstructed based on evidence from inventories and accounts, illuminated manuscripts, medieval artworks and antiquarian drawings. The room shows the King's bed, close to the fireplace for warmth, but allowing him a view of the little 'chapel over the water', mentioned in 13th-century records. The wall paintings are based on the floral 'pointing' described in accounts for Edward's mother's chamber at the Tower.

The travelling wardrobe

Because the court moved around the country so frequently, all the furnishings were of a type that could easily be dismantled and transported, as part of the King's travelling wardrobe. The textiles are woven with designs based on the royal arms of England, and of Edward's first wife, Eleanor of Castile. Sounds of conversation from the hall next door and the crackling of the fire can be heard, while Latin prayer in the oratory reminds us that this was a room for the King's private worship. The 13th-century stone basin for washing the vessels for Mass still survives. As king, Edward would have had fine, painted furniture, but on occasion he may have conducted private business in the bedchamber, and eaten on a small simple table attended by only his closest associates.

A covered bridge, built in the 19th century on the site of an earlier one, links Edward's Thomas's Tower to the Wakefield Tower, built by his father Henry III.

The small chapel, or oratory in the north-east turret of St Thomas's Tower. It was built for the king's private use.

The reconstructed throne room in the Wakefield Tower.

The Wakefield Tower

The Wakefield Tower was built by Henry III as royal lodgings between 1220 and 1240 and originally sat at the river's edge. Henry was able to arrive by boat, and enter his rooms from his private stairs leading from a postern gate.

The principal room was probably a private audience chamber. The replica throne and canopy are based on 13th-century examples. The pattern on the canopy and cushion features the Plantagenet lion – the symbol of the royal family. The painting on the chimney breast depicts the royal arms.

The vaulted ceiling is a 19th-century reconstruction. The fireplace and chapel are restored – the chapel screen is a copy of one very like that described in a detailed order by Henry '... and for making a good and suitable screen of wooden boards between the chamber and chapel of the new turret facing the Thames ... 16 pounds, 3 shillings and 8 pence'.

In the following century, the Wakefield Tower became one of the places in which to store the contents of the royal wardrobe, and royal residence shifted to the east of the castle. From 1870 until 1967 the Crown Jewels were displayed here.

In the 13th century, what we now call the Medieval Palace consisted of much more than St Thomas's and the Wakefield towers. The enclosed area in front of the White Tower is called the Inmost Ward. In the 1200s it was a busy complex, full of buildings set up to serve royal residence. These included kitchens and a great hall. The Inmost Ward was protected by a high wall and the enormous Coldharbour Gate-tower. Its foundations are to the left of the White Tower when facing north.

Medieval monarchs never stayed at the Tower for very long. Edward I, for example, only stayed here for 53 days in 35 years of rule.

The Lanthorn Tower

The Lanthorn Tower, built as part of Henry III's queen's lodgings, was gutted by fire in 1774. The present building is 19th century. Inside, a selection of 13th-century objects illustrate the lifestyle of Henry and Edward's courts.

Edward I's son Edward II (1307-27) stayed in this east side of the castle when in residence at the Tower. The Lanthorn Tower was eventually adapted into the king's chambers.

Henry VI

In 1471 Henry VI (r1422-61 and 1470-71) died as a prisoner during the Wars of the Roses, an event commemorated by a small plaque in the chapel floor in the Upper Wakefield Tower. One side said he died of melancholy after hearing his son had been killed in battle. His supporters, however, claimed he had been stabbed to death while praying. Since 1923 the 'Ceremony of the Lilies and Roses' has been held here every year on the evening of 21 May, the day of Henry's death, and is attended by representatives from Eton College and King's College Cambridge. Both these institutions were founded by the unfortunate King.

The Tower
Chapels

St John the Evangelist

Constructed as a place of worship for William the Conqueror, the Chapel of St John the Evangelist in the White Tower has had a long and surprising history.

Situated on the Tower's first floor, this elegant 11th-century chapel offers a highly decorated and impressive space suitable for royal worship. The barrel-vaulted roof and the upper gallery made it the highest room in the White Tower when first built, while the strikingly carved capitals on top of the pillars would have added further to its status and appearance.

The chapel would have been used by the royal family for worship while they were staying at the Tower. It's likely that the king himself would have sat on raised throne at the west end during services.

However, by the 13th century, the construction of other buildings for royal use meant that the chapel was used less frequently, and it gradually became a place to store important historic documents. It continued in this role for over 600 years before the documents were moved to the new Public Record Office.

With the documents removed, and with the encouragement of Queen Victoria's husband, the chapel was restored in the 1860s and resumed its role as a place of worship. At first it was used by non-conformist and Catholic members of the Tower's garrison, however, it is now used by all members of the community with regular monthly services.

St Peter ad Vincula

The Chapel Royal of St Peter ad Vincula is the Tower's parish church. It has been a site of worship since before the Tower was built.

It has witnessed all sides of community life and has served as a burial place for queens and saints, as well as Yeoman Warders and Mint workers.

The chapel was founded before the Norman invasion and the construction of the White Tower. Originally a church for local people, it was eventually taken within the Tower's walls and has acted as a place of religious worship for the men and women who lived and worked in the castle ever since.

The current building was erected around 1520 by Henry VIII, replacing an earlier chapel on the same site which had been destroyed by fire. Since then the interior has seen many additions and alterations with several monuments erected to the dead.

The chapel's most famous graves, however, had no markers until the 19th century, when the chapel was renovated. Under Henry VIII the chapel became the last resting place for many of the Tower's executed prisoners, such as Thomas More and Thomas Cromwell, as well as two of Henry's wives; Anne Boleyn and Catherine Howard. During the 1876 renovations, the area under the altar was excavated and the remains of several people were found. They were identified as high-status prisoners, including Anne Boleyn. The bodies were re-buried and their graves marked by marble slabs which can be seen today.

Left: the Norman Chapel of St John the Evangelist in the White Tower.

Right: The Holland Monument in the Chapel of St Peter was commissioned by John Holland, Constable of the Tower from 1420 to his death in 1447. It also contains the remains of at least two of his three wives. His favourite, Anne, lies next to him. The third figure may be his second wife or his sister Constance, with whom he also wished to be buried.

The Royal Menagerie

A terrible fight occurred in 1830 when a lion, tiger and tigress were accidently let into the same cage. Keepers managed to separate the animals, but not before the lion was 'so seriously injured that he died in a few days afterwards'.

For six hundred years, the Tower of London's most exotic prisoners were animals.

The Tower menagerie began as a result of medieval monarchs exchanging rare and strange animals as gifts. (Well, what do you give a monarch who has everything?) In 1235, Henry III was delighted to be presented with three wildcats by the Holy Roman Emperor Frederick II. These inspired the King to start a zoo at the Tower.

Henry's 'wildcats' although described as leopards, were probably lions, sent as a compliment to the Plantagenet arms that is made up of three lions. These are the ancestors of the three lions that still appear on the England football team's shirts today.

In 1252 the lions were joined by a 'white bear' – probably a polar bear – given by the king of Norway. This bear was allowed to swim in the Thames, at the end of a long leash, to catch fish. In 1255, the King of France sent the first elephant ever seen in England and 'people flocked together to see the novel sight'.

Sadly, the elephant died after two years in captivity. Poor treatment and cramped conditions meant that many of the lions and other animals did not survive for long. However, the Menagerie continued to grow, and an increasingly diverse collection of birds and beasts, including bears and apes were amassed.

Edward I (r1272–1307) created a permanent new home for the Menagerie at the western entrance to the Tower, in what became known as the Lion Tower. The terrifying sounds and smells of wild animals must have both impressed and intimidated visitors.

By 1622, the collection had been extended to include three eagles, two pumas, a tiger and a jackal, as well as lions and leopards, who were the main attractions.

In the early 17th century, James I had the lions' dens refurbished. Visitors could look down into a semi-circular yard lined with dens and see the 'greate cisterne ...for the Lyons to drinke and washe themselfes in'. However, this was less out of a concern for their welfare, as James's favourite sport was to bait the lions with vicious mastiff dogs.

Occasionally the beasts had their revenge. A female leopard would seize umbrellas, parasols, muffs and hats from visitors with 'the greatest quickness' before 'tearing them into pieces', and the 'school of monkeys' was disbanded when one of its members 'tore a boy's leg'. In 1686, Mary Jenkinson died after an encounter with one of the lions. She tried to stroke him, he pounced, and her death followed on from the botched amputation of her mauled arm.

At the beginning of the 19th century, the menagerie was in decline, until it was revitalised by the energetic zoologist Alfred Cops, Head Keeper. He acquired over 300 specimens and rekindled the popularity of the Tower as a tourist attraction.

In 1252 the lions were joined by a 'white bear' – probably a polar bear – given by the King of Norway. This bear was allowed to swim in the Thames, at the end of a long leash, to catch fish.

Polar bear sculpture in Water Lane by Kendra Haste.

The Tower ravens

Legend says that the kingdom and the Tower will fall if the six resident ravens ever leave the fortress. It was Charles II, according to the stories, who first insisted that the ravens of the Tower be protected.

The kingdom did not in fact fall when the ravens were temporarily absent during the disruption of the Second World War, but it seems foolish to take chances. Today the Tower's seven ravens (one spare) are looked after very carefully by the Ravenmaster. They eat 170g (6oz) of raw meat a day, plus bird biscuits soaked in blood. They enjoy an egg once a week, the occasional rabbit (complete with fur) and scraps of fried bread. Some of them are fond of crisps, too, but please don't feed them!

However, the end of the menagerie came in the 1830s. Campaigners (the Royal Society for the Prevention of Cruelty to Animals was founded in 1824) had begun to raise concerns, and the animals were expensive, occasionally dangerous and a nuisance to the garrison. The Duke of Wellington, who became Constable of the Tower in 1826, despatched 150 of the beasts to a new zoo in Regent's Park; today's London Zoo.

Despite Cops's best efforts to carry on, several further incidents including an escaped wolf and a monkey that bit a guardsman's leg, convinced King William IV to close the Menagerie for good in 1835. The remaining animals were sold to zoos and travelling shows, and the Lion Tower was later demolished.

Illustrations from *Curiosities in the Tower of London*, a children's guidebook published in 1741, showing animals in the Menagerie.

Halt!
Who Comes There?

While the Tower remains a living fortress, changing and adapting as times demand, it still maintains centuries of colourful traditions.

The Ceremony of the Keys

'Halt! Who comes there?' These familiar words echo down Water Lane every night as they have done for over 700 years. They are part of the ancient Ceremony of the Keys in which the outer gates of the fortress are locked for the night and the keys delivered to the monarch's representative in the Tower, the Resident Governor. The ceremony is open to the public by application in advance*.

Beating the Bounds

The area around the Tower, including Tower Hill, known as the Tower Liberty, is controlled by the Tower but its borders have been disputed with the City of London for centuries. It is marked by boundary stones and every three years on Ascension Day, local children and officials walk the streets around the Tower and beat the stones with willow wands. This dates back to a 14th-century tradition that boys were actually beaten at the stones so they would remember their location!

The Constable's Dues

The 'Dues' are one of several perks that the Constable of the Tower traditionally enjoyed. Every ship that came upstream to the City had to moor at Tower Wharf to unload a portion of its cargo for the Constable. Still today, whenever a Royal Naval vessel moors on the Wharf the Captain must present the Constable with a barrel of wine (the 'Dues'). This is ceremoniously escorted into the Tower by the Yeoman Warders and presented to the Constable on Tower Green.

A ship's crew, escorted by a Yeoman Warder, deliver the ceremonial 'Dues' to the Constable of the Tower.

The Bounds-Beating party assembled on Tower Green in 1924, willow wands at the ready.

Gun salutes

One of the first recorded royal salutes to be fired from the Tower of London was on Whit Sunday 1533 to mark the coronation of Anne Boleyn, Henry VIII's second wife. Since then gun salutes have marked a variety of occasions including the Union of Great Britain and Ireland in 1800 and the opening of Tower Bridge in 1894. Today, 62-gun salutes are fired for royal occasions, including The Queen's birthday and on the anniversary of her accession to the throne, and 41-gun salutes are fired at the State Opening of Parliament. Royal births are always celebrated and gun salutes were fired for Prince George in 2013 and Princess Charlotte in 2015**.

The Ceremony of the Lilies & Roses

By tradition, the chapel in the Wakefield Tower is linked to the death of King Henry VI in 1471 after he was imprisoned in the Tower during the Wars of the Roses. Henry may have been murdered while at prayer in the Wakefield Tower chapel, although his rivals claimed he died from melancholy. His supporters claimed he was 'stykked with a dagger' by Richard, Duke of Gloucester (later King Richard III). Each year, on the anniversary of his death, representatives of Eton College and King's College Cambridge, both of which Henry founded, lay lilies and roses on the spot where he is said to have died.

*To apply for tickets to the Ceremony of the Keys visit **www.hrp.org.uk**

For dates and times of all gun salutes visit **www.hrp.org.uk

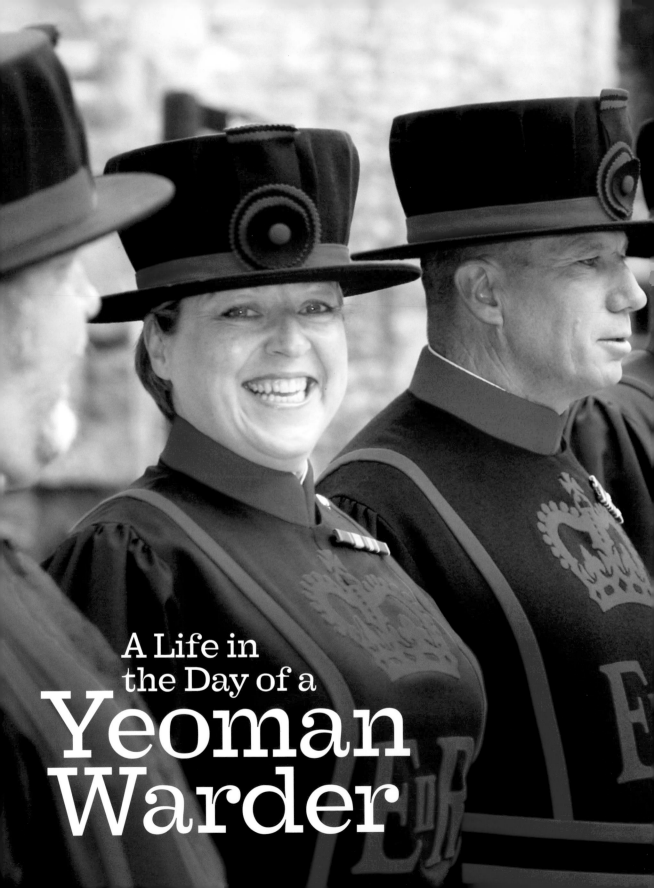

A Life in
the Day of a
Yeoman
Warder

I had to get up at 5.30am this morning, as my partner David was leaving for work in Pimlico. There's such a different feel about the Tower at that time in the morning; the ravens are out and squawking away on top of the Martin Tower, and you can only just hear the distant traffic. I feel like I'm cushioned inside the walls, safe and secure in the fortress.

I started work around 6.30am, when I opened up the Middle Drawbridge so that people leaving the Tower could drive out, and delivery vans can get in. We are a little community here; you get to know everyone so it's a nice time to say hello and to wave people off to work.

Apart from the Warders and their families, some with very young children, we have a Chaplain, Resident Governor and a Doctor who live on site. Members of various regiments of the Queen's Guards (the ones in the bearskins) come to stay for short periods. They guard the Queen's House and the Crown Jewels, and also perform ceremonial duties at St James's Palace and Buckingham Palace.

I really enjoy the interaction with people … A little boy came up to me recently and asked, 'Can you be my history teacher?' What a compliment!

This morning I was on early guided tours, kicking off at 10am with the first one of the day, with two more to do later on. Each of us on tour duty has to lead three tours a day, which last about an hour each.

A Yeoman Warder has six months to learn the standard script of the Tower's history off by heart. Then at the end of training, you have to perform for the Chief Yeoman Warder and the Resident Governor first thing in the morning. The tradition is that if you pass you have to take the first public guided tour of the day, which is really nerve-wracking! After that you can adapt the script, dropping or expanding points to make it your own while staying factually correct.

I really enjoy the interaction with people. Every group of visitors is different. Some ask a lot of questions, other times everyone is silent, only for you to find at the end they are the most appreciative of all and they've absorbed every word! A little boy came up to me recently and asked, 'Can you be my history teacher!' What a compliment!

Moira Cameron, the Tower's first female Yeoman Warder. Her appointment in July 2007 made headlines around the world.

If I'm not doing tour duty my first job of the day, along with my colleagues, is to open all five 'inner circuit' posts (where the Yeoman Warders stand) and check all is clean, tidy and safe for visitors. We then each take a position for an hour before moving round, with a quick cup of tea in between! We help and guide visitors, look out for any problems and pose for what seems like millions of photographs! In the summer up to 17,000 people a day visit the Tower, so we have to stay alert and keep smiling!

My uniform is just the same as the men's, with a few adjustments. For normal duty we wear the blue 'undress' uniform, and on ceremonial occasions, we wear the red full State uniform. While it looks splendid and I am incredibly proud to wear it, I have to say it's the most uncomfortable uniform I've ever worn in my life! The material is really thick and the ruff doesn't allow you much movement.

You need someone to help you the first time you wear the full uniform. It has to be put on in order, as you can't bend down once that thick, cumbersome tunic is on. So it's a thin T-shirt first, then the special tights, then breeches. Your ruff goes on back to front, then you have to push it round (not too quickly or you'll garrotte yourself) before putting on the tunic which has tightly fastening buttons up the side, really hard to reach. Then belt, sword, partisan (ceremonial spear) and gloves, then finally Tudor bonnet.

The evening routine is to help with the wind-down, doing a security sweep of the whole fortress, ensuring everyone has left. Some nights I take my turn to perform the Ceremony of the Keys (see page 62), or occasionally I am invited to speak at a corporate function at the Tower. But I love an evening when there is no one around, the ravens are in bed, and I can feel the Tower relaxing, away from the public gaze. 'Putting its slippers on', as I like to think of it.

Moira Cameron
Yeoman Warder

Moira Cameron was the first female Yeoman Warder at the Tower of London. She joined on 1 July, 2007. She now has the additional role of Clerk to the Chapels Royal, and she lives in a subsidised apartment in Casemates at the Tower, as do the other Yeoman Warders and their families.

Yeoman Warders need to have at least 22 years' military service; to have reached the rank of Warrant Officer; to have been awarded the Long Service and Good Conduct Medal and to be between 40 and 55 years old on appointment.

Prison

The Tower as Prison

Although the Tower wasn't built as a prison, between 1100 and 1952 hundreds of people were incarcerated here. Over the centuries, a potent mix of legend, fact and fiction has created the Tower's fearsome reputation. Eventually, the fortress was no longer used to contain enemies of the state and became principally a secure store for documents, armaments and priceless jewels. However, it remained best known as a dark place of execution and torture.

It's not hard to understand why the Tower's fearsome spell has gripped the popular imagination, particularly since it grew in popularity as a tourist attraction in the 19th century. Victorian crowds, entranced by the dark, the gothic, and exaggerated accounts of torture and bloody execution, flocked to the fortress to enjoy an agreeable chill in the 'dungeons' and to view the ominous ravens perched on medieval stonework. Visitors were fascinated, as we still are today, by the terrible fates of prisoners arriving through Traitors' Gate, and by visualising the executions on Tower Green.

However, this popular image is only part of the story. Many people suffered horribly at the Tower, bodies and minds broken through torture and years of incarceration, but there was in reality a huge variety of prisoner experience. A number of royal and high status prisoners enjoyed relative luxury at the Tower, deprived only of their freedom while waited on by their servants and supplied with plentiful food and alcohol by members of their wealthy families. The cries of poorer, less influential prisoners, losing hope after years locked in less well-appointed cells, probably never reached their ears.

The first prisoner, Ranulf Flambard, a bishop accused of extortion, escaped in 1100. Among the last prisoners at the Tower were notorious London gangsters Ronald and Reginald Kray, held in 1952 for failing to report for compulsory (military) National Service. In the eight centuries in between, thousands of men and women were held for a variety of crimes, but the majority were prisoners of war and those imprisoned for their religious beliefs and political allegiances.

Torture was used, but the recorded number of cases is surprisingly small. It was mainly used to elicit information, rather than as a punishment, but it was real enough. Even just the threat of the agony to come was sometimes enough to break a prisoner's resolve. John Gerard, a Jesuit priest imprisoned in the Tower during Elizabeth I's reign described being shown a 'torture room … every device and instrument of torture was there. They pointed out some of them to me and said I would try them all.'

The block and axe reputedly used to behead Simon Fraser, 11th Lord Lovat in 1747. He was 80, and the last person to be executed on Tower Hill.

Father John Gerard, a Jesuit priest, was imprisoned in the Tower during the reign of Protestant Elizabeth I. He was tortured twice (he is shown here suspended in manacles in the White Tower), but he later escaped from the Tower. He used orange juice as invisible ink to send messages to his friends.

Sent
to
the Tower

Sir Thomas More was imprisoned in the Bell Tower in 1534 after refusing to acknowledge Henry VIII's supremacy over the Church. He was executed on Tower Hill the following year. Here, he is depicted saying farewell to his daughter in a painting by William Frederick Yeames, 1863.

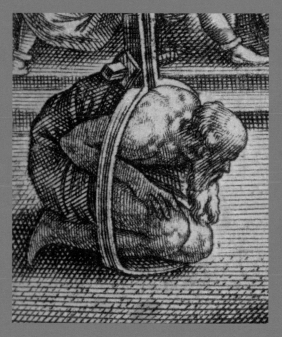

The torture device known as 'Scavenger's Daughter' was reputedly so painful that victims could withstand no more than an hour.

The Tower of London is soaked with the bloody history of England's dynastic and foreign wars. Hundreds have entered this place, only to leave for a miserable march to a place of execution outside the Tower.

Tower Hill

Most Tower prisoners sentenced to death were executed on Tower Hill, outside the Tower walls. Nobles were beheaded; 'ordinary' people were hanged. The site of the scaffold is marked by a memorial in Trinity Gardens at the top of the hill, which lists around 30 'noble' names. However, we now know that around 440 people were killed on or near that site, the majority of whom were members of the Jewish community of the 1270s. Many of those persecuted spent their last night at the Tower.

Tower Green

By comparison with the public executions on Tower Hill, only a small number of 'controversial' killings took place within the Tower's walls. These were easier to control within the fortress. Ten people were executed – seven beheaded and three shot – out of the public gaze on this peaceful green that stretches to the west of the White Tower. Three of those who lost their heads were English queens.

Anne Boleyn, the second wife of Henry VIII, was in her early 30s; Catherine Howard, Henry's fifth wife, barely in her 20s: both had been accused of adultery; neither may have been guilty. Lady Jane Grey, queen for nine days, was only 16, the innocent pawn in a failed military coup by her father-in-law, the Duke of Northumberland.

Social convention ensured that right up until the end they were treated in the manner befitting their status. 'Shall I go into a dungeon?' Anne had asked on her arrival at the Tower. 'No, madam', came the reply, 'You shall go into the lodging that you lay in at your coronation.' The irony was keenly felt. She was executed by a clean stroke of an expert swordsman specially imported from France.

> Lady Jane Grey and her husband Lord Guildford Dudley were both executed at the Tower. She saw his decapitated body from her window an hour before she was beheaded on Tower Green.

The last moments of Lady Jane Grey, as imagined by 19th-century artist Hendrik Jacobus Scholten, c1845.

The Execution Site Memorial sculpture. The granite and glass sculpture created by Brian Catling shows a crystal pillow resting on two polished discs.

Memorial to the dead

The actual site for all three of these executions was different – with a special scaffold and block being prepared each time – but all took place close to where the present Execution Site Memorial sculpture is now positioned. This memorial also recalls the death of the other men and women on or near this spot.

Those remembered are Jane Boleyn, Viscountess Rochford (and erstwhile sister-in-law to Anne Boleyn) who died alongside Catherine Howard. As Catherine's lady-in-waiting, she was complicit in the Queen's alleged adultery. Margaret Pole, the 67-year old Countess of Salisbury, was executed by Henry VIII for her supposed involvement in a Catholic invasion. A blundering executioner 'hacked her head and shoulders to pieces'. Royal favourite Robert Devereux, Earl of Essex, was also executed away from public gaze, on the orders of Elizabeth I. The authorities supplied two axes to ensure the job was done properly.

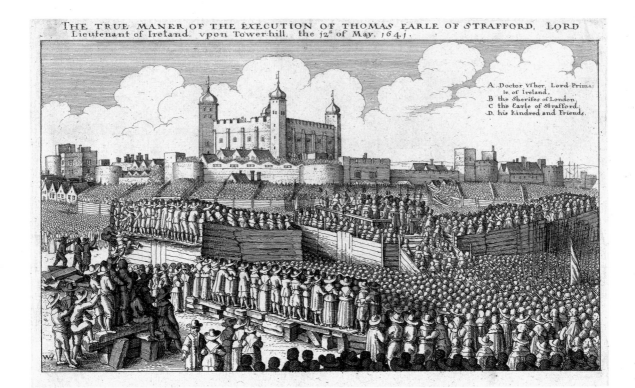

THE TRUE MANER OF THE EXECUTION OF THOMAS EARLE OF STRAFFORD, LORD Lieutenant of Ireland. vpon Tower-hill, the 12ᵗ of May, 1641.

A. Doctor Vsher, Lord Prima-
te of Ireland,
B. the Sherifes of London,
C. the Earle of Strafford,
D. his Kindred and Friends.

This contemporary engraving shows the crowds gathered on Tower Hill for the execution of Lord Strafford in 1641.

Era of executions

These royally directed executions were committed within the bloody century of Tudor rule, between 1536 and 1601. They are book-ended by the deaths of four more men, whose guilt was also thoroughly questionable. William, Lord Hastings, was beheaded in 1483 probably on the orders of Richard of Gloucester, who was in the process of a messy take-over of the throne - to become the infamous King Richard III. Much later, in 1743, Farquhar Shaw and the cousins Samuel and Malcolm Macpherson were shot at dawn on Tower Green in front of the rest of their regiment, the 'Black Watch', for being ringleaders in a so-called mutiny.

The three English queens, and Lords Rochford, Salisbury and Essex are all buried in the Chapel Royal of St Peter ad Vincula (see also page 56). They share their burial place with other famous prisoners of the Tower, including two saints of the Roman Catholic Church, Thomas More and John Fisher (who were executed on Tower Hill).

The bigger picture

But the history of imprisonment at the Tower is a much longer story. The first prisoner arrived at the Tower on Wednesday 15 August 1100. Ranulf Flambard had been Bishop of Durham and chief tax-gatherer for William II. Under the new king, Henry I, he was accused of extortion and hauled off to the White Tower in chains. Over 800 years later, on 15 August 1941, Josef Jakobs was the last of 12 men shot by firing squad at the Tower, guilty of spying for Germany during the Second World War. In between, the Tower was home to kings and queens, priests and heretics, Welsh, Scottish, French, German and American prisoners of war, thieves and politicians, terrorists and soldiers, aristocrats and prostitutes.

Most royally-directed executions were committed during the bloody century of Tudor rule, between 1536 and 1601.

The Beauchamp Tower and prisoner graffiti

The Tower of London was not constructed as a prison, and there were no purpose-built cells. Prisoners were squeezed in anywhere. The Beauchamp Tower to the west of Tower Green is part of the inner defensive wall built by Henry III and Edward I around the White Tower. But the tower takes its name from Thomas Beauchamp, Earl of Warwick, who was imprisoned there at the end of the 14th century. The Beauchamp Tower has been used to house prisoners, off and on, throughout its history, and its walls are covered in the graffiti they left behind. The Beauchamp now contains an exhibition that gives an overview of the prisoners at the Tower.

The vast majority of inscriptions date from the 16th and 17th centuries, when political and religious instability combined to establish the Tower as the foremost state prison in the country. Many of those accused of treason were guilty of nothing more than ending up on the losing side of one of the country's bitter and complex dynastic wars.

When power lay exclusively within the upper ranks of society, it was virtually impossible to be a nobleman without committing to one particular side or another. The acutely tetchy Tudors were particularly keen to keep rivals to the throne locked up.

Of course, there were genuine causes of concern. The Tudor dynasty's claim to power was notoriously weak, and bringing the Reformation to England didn't help stability. Being Protestant or Catholic became not only a statement of conscience but also frequently a declaration of political allegiance. There were plots to replace Mary I with Elizabeth I, and plots to replace Elizabeth I with practically any suitable Catholic alternative. Philip Howard, Earl of Arundel, was imprisoned in the Beauchamp Tower for ten years by Elizabeth, for no other obvious reason than being the leading Catholic peer in the country.

Under Elizabeth I, it was illegal simply to be a Roman Catholic priest in England; many were arrested and charged with treason. Some found safety in exile, others died traitors' deaths: hanged, drawn and quartered, many after interrogation and torture.

Sir Philip Howard, Earl of Arundel languished in the Beauchamp Tower for ten years until he died in 1595.

The identification of an actual site responds in part to a need in all of us to find a focus, a sense of 'history where it happened' which previous Tower authorities have been more than happy to satisfy. (See page 14 for more on the Princes.)

The more prosaic truth of this particular tower is that it was originally called the Garden Tower and was a secure 'home' for many years to Sir Walter Ralegh, where although a prisoner, he was often visited by his family. Ralegh wrote his unfinished *History of the World* here, and conducted scientific experiments in the adjacent gardens.

Imprisonment at the Tower of London has varied from the luxurious to the lethal. Some certainly enjoyed particularly comfortable 'imprisonments'. King John the Good of France enjoyed a royal diet, and the company of a section of his court, including an organist and 'Master John the Fool'. But for many others, the reality of imprisonment was grim indeed: physical torture; mental anguish, and the threat of a trial or immediate execution.

Eventually, the Tower's infamy and popularity as a visitor attraction outgrew its usefulness as a prison. The days of being locked up for your religious views, or on the tyrannical whim of a paranoid ruler, are – thankfully – over. Aren't they?

The Lower Wakefield Tower

Today this tower provides a short account of the history of torture at the Tower, although it is not where torture actually occurred. It takes its name from more than 200 prisoners of war that were held here in 1460 after the Battle of Wakefield, in West Yorkshire.

Only a tiny fraction of prisoners held at the Tower were tortured. Torture was essentially part of a carefully designed programme of interrogation, and only used to elicit information or to persuade the prisoner to sign a written statement to be used in law. It was, nonetheless, barbarically cruel, and – perhaps more importantly to the authorities who abandoned its use in the 17th century – often unreliable.

The Bloody Tower

Nonetheless, the Tower of London has acquired a reputation as a ruthless executor of state power. It is almost as if the very stones have developed a taste for murder. The Bloody Tower of popular imagination is a good example of this. From as long ago as the early 1600s it was believed to be the place where the 'Princes in the Tower' had been murdered by their uncle, Richard III. However, there is nothing in any of the accounts that identify the Bloody Tower as the scene for the supposed crime.

King John II of France, fortunate among the Tower's prisoners, enjoyed a royal diet and the company of several members of his court.

The Garden Tower, later more dramatically named 'Bloody Tower', usually housed wealthy prisoners like Sir Walter Ralegh in suites of rooms like this that were well furnished and relatively spacious.

A reconstruction of Sir Walter Ralegh's comfortable study, in the Bloody Tower.

Famous Prisoners
(And the not-so-famous)

Along with the well-known inmates, an American president, a bishop and a poet were among those incarcerated at the Tower.

Anne Askew
(1521-46)

The only woman known to have been tortured at the Tower. In 1546, 25-year-old Anne was accused of being a Protestant heretic. She was tortured on the rack repeatedly as she refused to confess or to name fellow Protestants. Sentenced to death, she was later carried, as she was unable to walk after torture, to be burnt at the stake.

Ranulf Flambard
(d1128)

Bishop of Durham and King William II's chief tax collector

Imprisoned in the White Tower in 1100-1, for corruption. Flambard was the Tower's first high-profile prisoner and its first escapee: a rope was smuggled to him in a gallon of wine; he got his guards drunk and used the rope to escape.

Sir William de la Pole
(1478-1539)

English nobleman

Sir William, a distant relative of King Henry VIII, was incarcerated at the Tower for 37 years until his death in 1539, making him the longest-held prisoner at the fortress. He was accused of plotting against King Henry VII but the evidence was flimsy.

Princess Elizabeth
(1533-1603)

Daughter of King Henry VIII and future Queen Elizabeth I

Imprisoned by her half-sister, Queen Mary I, in 1554 on suspicion of plotting against her, the Princess (above left) was granted spacious accommodation and was allowed to walk in the gardens during her confinement. After a few weeks she was put under house arrest in the country.

Lady Jane Grey (1537-54)

Queen of England for nine days

Lady Jane Grey was proclaimed Queen of England in July 1553 – and became a prisoner at the Tower of London just days later, the result of an unsuccessful bid to prevent the accession of the Catholic Mary Tudor. Jane was executed on Tower Green on 12 February 1554.

Sir Walter Ralegh (c1552-1618)

Adventurer and favourite of Queen Elizabeth I

Imprisoned three times: in 1592 for marrying one of the Queen's ladies-in-waiting without her permission; in 1603-16 for conspiring against King James I and trying to place the King's cousin, Lady Arabella Stuart on the throne; and in 1618 for deliberately inciting war between Spain and England. Ralegh was executed in Old Palace Yard, Westminster on 29 October 1618.

Guy Fawkes (1570-1606)

Conspirator in the failed Gunpowder Plot

On 5 November 1605, Fawkes was caught red-handed with 36 barrels of gunpowder and matches in a cellar beneath the Houses of Parliament. He was taken to the Tower, interrogated then tortured, probably on the rack. He eventually confessed and was sentenced to a traitor's death of hanging, drawing and quartering.

Sir Thomas Overbury (1581-1613)

English poet and author

Overbury suffered a prolonged and agonizing death by poison while a prisoner in the Bloody Tower. He had tried in vain to dissuade his friend the Earl of Somerset from marrying the evil Frances Howard. In revenge, she used her influence with King James I to have Overbury imprisoned and finally contrived his murder.

Henry Laurens (1724-92)

President of the American Congress

The first and last United States citizen to be imprisoned at the Tower. Laurens was held on suspicion of high treason for his part in the American struggle for independence from Great Britain and became a prisoner of state for more than a year.

Rudolf Hess (1894-1987)

Deputy Führer to Adolf Hitler

Hess was one of the last state prisoners to be held at the Tower. He was imprisoned in the Queen's House in 1941 after crash-landing his plane in Scotland. After four days of interrogation he was removed from the Tower and spent the rest of the war as a prisoner at Mytchett Place in Surrey.

Kings and Queens of England

House of Normandy

William I	1066–1087
William II	1087–1100
Henry I	1100–1135
Stephen	1135–1154

House of Plantagenet

Henry II	1154–1189
Richard I	1189–1199
John	1199–1216
Henry III	1216–1272
Edward I	1272–1307
Edward II	1307–1327
Edward III	1327–1377
Richard II	1377–1399
Henry IV	1399–1413
Henry V	1413–1422
Henry VI	1422–1461
	1470–1471
Edward IV	1461–1470
	1471–1483
Edward V	1483
Richard III	1483–1485

House of Tudor

Henry VII	1485–1509
Henry VIII	1509–1547
Edward VI	1547–1553
Mary I	1553–1558
Elizabeth I	1558–1603

House of Stuart

James I	1603–1625
Charles I	1625–1649
The Commonwealth	1649–1660
Charles II	1660–1685
James II	1685–1688
William III & Mary II	1689–1702
Anne*	1702–1714

House of Hanover

George I	1714–1727
George II	1727–1760
George III	1760–1820
George IV	1820–1830
William IV	1830–1837
Victoria	1837–1901

House of Saxe–Coburg

Edward VII	1901–1910

House of Windsor

George V	1910–1936
Edward VIII	1936
George VI	1936–1952
Elizabeth II	Succeeded 1952

* First monarch of Great Britain

Join us!

We have five more fabulous palaces to explore – why not take out a membership of Historic Royal Palaces and enjoy them all, as many times as you like in a year?

As a member of Historic Royal Palaces, you will enjoy:

- Unlimited access to all our palaces

- 10% discount in our palace shops, online store, cafes and restaurants

- Free subscription to our members' magazine, *Inside Story*

- An exciting programme of exclusive member events

For more about visiting all our palaces and our inspiring events and exhibitions throughout the year, visit **www.hrp.org.uk**

Membership makes a great gift, too, for someone with a love of history, extraordinary buildings and fascinating collections. It offers amazing value, too.

For more information on individual, family and gift memberships please visit **www.hrp.org.uk/ membership** or call us on **0203 166 6327.**

Thank you for playing your part

Historic Royal Palaces looks after the Tower of London, Hampton Court Palace, the Banqueting House, Kensington Palace, Kew Palace and Hillsborough Castle and Gardens.

We are an independent charity and generate all our own funds. We rely on the support of our visitors, members, donors, sponsors and volunteers. By visiting the palace today, and by purchasing this guidebook, you are helping us to give the palaces we care for a future as bright as their past.

Discover more about Historic Royal Palaces and how to get involved in what we do at **www.hrp.org.uk/support-us**

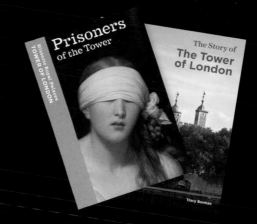

Discover more about the Tower of London at **www.hrp.org.uk**

And visit our online shop at **www.historicroyalpalaces.com** for our full range of books and beautiful gifts inspired by centuries of stories from six amazing palaces.

The Story of the Tower
Tracy Borman
Merrell Publishers in association with Historic Royal Palaces, 2015

The Official Crown Jewels Guidebook
Historic Royal Palaces, 2018

The Crown Jewels
Anna Keay
Thames & Hudson, 2011

Prisoners of the Tower
Jeremy Ashbee *et al*
Historic Royal Palaces, 2004

The Really Useful Guide to Kings and Queens of England
Chris Gidlow *et al*
Historic Royal Palaces, 2011

Terrible True Tales from the Tower of London
Sarah Kilby
Historic Royal Palaces, 2017

For young children:
Tower Power: Tales from the Tower of London
Historic Royal Palaces, 2018

Acknowledgements

Published by Historic Royal Palaces
Hampton Court Palace
Surrey KT8 9AU
© Historic Royal Palaces, 2019

ISBN   978-1-873993-38-5

Written by Tracy Borman (Tower History), Sarah Kilby, Clare Murphy, Alden Gregory (White Tower and the Lost Tudor Palace), Megan Gooch (Treasure Chest) George Roberts (Chapels) and Jane Spooner (Medieval Palace). Additional research by Sally Dixon-Smith.

Edited by Sarah Kilby and Clare Murphy

Picture research Susan Mennell

Designed by Open Agency

Historic Royal Palaces is the charity that looks after:

Tower of London
Hampton Court Palace
Banqueting House
Kensington Palace
Kew Palace
Hillsborough Castle

We help everyone explore the story of how monarchs and people have shaped society, in some of the greatest palaces ever built.

We raise all our own funds and depend on the support of our visitors, members, donors, sponsors and volunteers.

Principal photography by James Brittain
Front cover photography by Eric Richmond and James Brittain
Illustration page 6 by Ivan Lapper
Illustration page 8 by Edward Impey
Illustrations inside back cover by Robin Wyatt
Printed by CPI Colour Ltd

Illustrations:
Unless otherwise indicated, all illustrations are © Historic Royal Palaces.
For illustrations that are © Historic Royal Palaces, please visit our online Image Library (www.images.hrp.org.uk)

Front cover: © Historic Royal Palaces

© The Trustees of the British Museum: pp 15bl, 44c, 44br, 45t, 45br, 72; Bridgeman Images: Contents (detail), pp 4r, 21, 26l, 26r, 58-59, 61r (Royal Armouries, Leeds, UK); p 15t (Museum of London); 16b (London Metropolitan Archives, City of London); pp 10, 11, 12-13, 25, 28-29, 34-35, 35t, 43, 47, 53, 66, 69 (© British Library Board. All rights reserved); pp 37bl, 37br (© Leeds Museums and Galleries); p 74t (His Grace the Duke of Norfolk, Arundel Castle); p 77c (Tatton Park, Cheshire); p 36tl (Westminster Abbey, London); Geoffrey Parnell: p 9; Crown copyright: Historic Royal Palaces: pp 19tr, 19b, 37t, 48-49; Historic Royal Palaces Yeoman Warder Archive: p 19tl, 19br; Imperial War Museum, London: 77cr; Museum of London (by kind permission of St Gregory's Church, Sudbury, Suffolk): p 36b; Image © Ministry of Defence, Crown Copyright 2018: p 17b; © National Portrait Gallery, London: pp 7, 38, 51, 55b, 77tl, 77c; The Royal Collection Trust © 2018 Her Majesty Queen Elizabeth II: pp 4l, 15br, 39, 40-41, 42, 43t, 50, 76l; The Royal Mint: pp 44tl, 45c; © Stratfield Saye Preservation Trust: p 16t; © Telegraph Media Group Limited 2017: p 64; Topfoto (Fotomas): pp 27, 44-45, 77c (detail); US Senate Collection: 77tr.

The exhibition 'Crowns Through History' has been made possible by the generosity of De Beers Group of Companies. Their contribution is gratefully acknowledged.

www.hrp.org.uk

 @HRP_palaces

 /Historic Royal Palaces

 youtube.com/HistoricRoyalPalaces